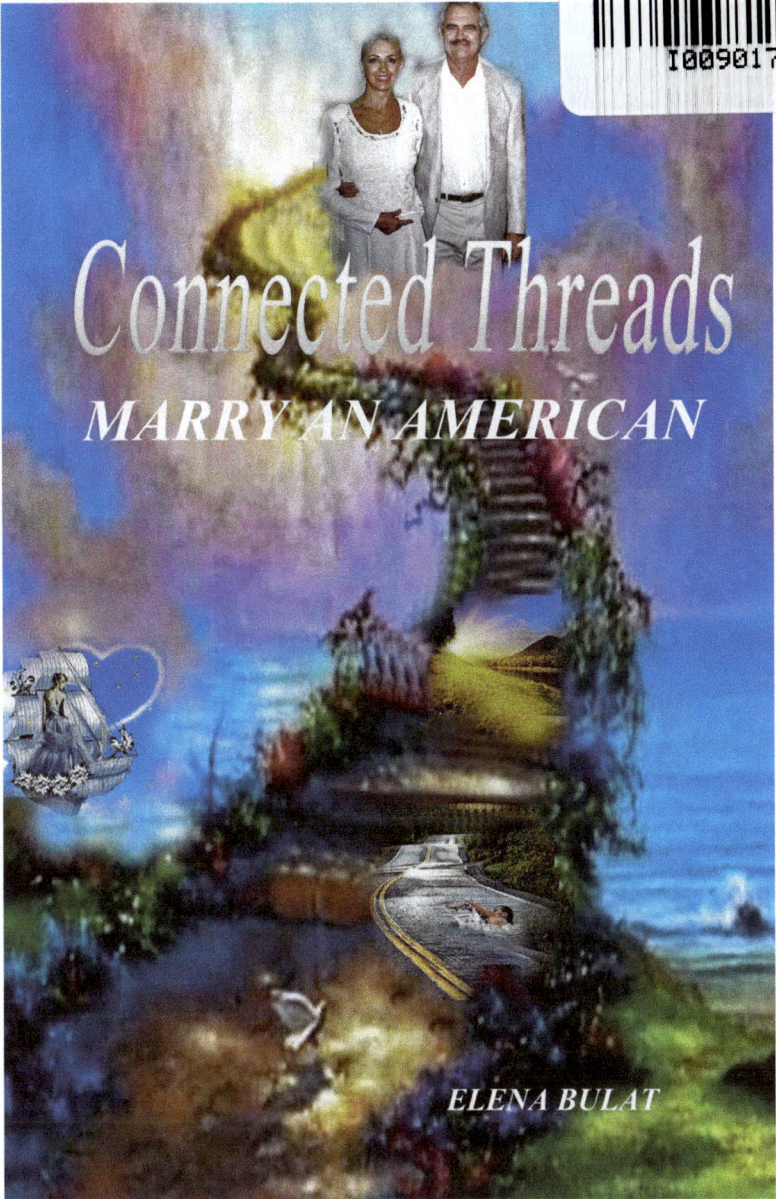

Connected Threads

MARRY AN AMERICAN

ELENA BULAT

978-1-950311-64-4

CONNECTED THREADS

Marry an American

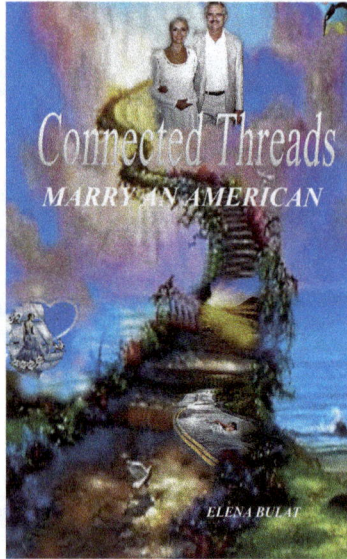

Elena Bulat

ISBN-13: 978-1-950311-64-4

Disclaimer

"This book has form of an autobiography, but it is not one. It reflects the author's present recollections of experiences over time. Some names and characteristics have been changed, some events have been compressed, and some dialogue has been recreated.

The book does not describe specific individuals. Space and time have been rearranged to suit the convenience of the book, and any resemblance to persons living or dead is coincidental. The opinions expressed are those of the characters and should not be confused with the author's.

The text, characters and plot of this book could take place anywhere in the world. It cannot be used against anybody or in the court of law. It is only a creation of the writer."

Every movement is a dance of life, if you decide to move.
Love is only your Life
The Walking One Will Overpower Any Road...

Contents

Read: www.TangoCaminito.com

About Book

At all times, people ask the eternal question of the meaning of life, "how to live and what to do." Everyone wants to find happiness, sometimes without answering what it means for one. In different periods of life, each person can be happy for various reasons. Some people at any age have strength and desire to start a new life, meet love and be happy. There is practically nothing that cannot be overcome if a person sets goals and tries to achieve them, no matter what.

This book is about a strange game of fate. The threads of some events began back in the nineteenth century. Hundred years later, they came to their logical conclusion. Invisible, connecting threads sped to the other end of the earth, across the ocean, continuing to weave the paths of fate, connecting the past with the future. The whirlwinds of fate weaved the lives of a Soviet woman Alena and American man Victusha, invisible threads connected impossible destinies together.

The book tells about a woman Alena who, on a bet, moved to America, how she lived there, looking for her happiness under different circumstances and conditions. Miraculous transformations came to Alena with her belief in her happiness, which filled her soul with joy.

To feel peace of mind, one needs to focus on the positive aspects of each day. Throwing any negative husks aside, it is important to notice all the best in the person who lives nearby. The law of happiness is to collect the grains of joy of every day, string them like beads on the threads of events, and always carry a joyful necklace of happiness with you.

Once Alena realized that if a person has any problems their resolution must be sought in childhood events. At the same time, she understood that happiness is always within oneself. To feel peace of mind, one needs to focus on the positive aspects of each day. Throwing any negative husks aside, it is important to notice all the best in the person who lives nearby. The law of happiness is to collect the grains of joy of every day, string them like beads on the threads of events, and always carry a joyful necklace of happiness with you. One people's wisdom is to remember: protect your love when you met it.

***

Milestones

From the age of seventeen Alena lived on her own. She lost her relatives very early and survived many difficult trials. Many worries were on her shoulder, but she was not afraid of them. Alena's character was persistent, and she fought as best she could, no matter what. Her daughter also got married and divorced early, and Alena needed to help her to raise a child. Believing in her success, luck and happiness, Alena was ready to overcome everything, in order to find a path to a better life.

In the alarming 1990s, during revolutionary changes in the country, the Russian state was falling apart. At the same time, vigorous and prosperous entrepreneurs (new Russians) were attacked by bandits and racketeers. Despite the difficult situation of the inhabitants of Russia, Alena's life was flourishing. She, as they say, "raked money with a shovel" from a new business which she created with the help of friends. It seemed to her that she was happy during the bustle of this notorious "perestroika".

By the age of forty, Alena had already traveled to many countries, and decided that it was time to fulfill her long-held dream and move to live somewhere abroad. Moreover, for many years, special portents and coincidences told her that this would be a good solution. Alena wanted to overcome the most implausible path and find out if she could live in America, a country inaccessible to the majority of Russian people. Alena planned to live in warm California, by the ocean, where the climate was similar to the climate of her hometown on the Black Sea. In any case, she believed in the power of her beauty, and in the fact that she was lucky to do everything that she had in mind.

At first, in a new country, she was curious, and everything was new and interesting. But like other foreigners, she went through several stages of adaptation to a new civilization. It was difficult for many immigrants to find friends, work, something close to their heart in the new world. For a long time, Alena did not know what to do and how to live. She was constantly yearning for her past busy life. She began to realize that she was really happy when she worked as a guide in her beloved St. Petersburg, when everything was more joyful. But in her home land, everything and everybody was already lost and dead. And in her new life for a long time there was no inner peace, no meaning of life and contentment.

She could not live in a state of discomfort or without love. So, soon she found in herself the strength to radically change everything again, starting from scratch. This time a miracle happened. Alena met an amazing man and married him. But living in a large house on a hill, surrounded by continuous tangerine-avocado plantations, she yearned for society, and again strove for an active life. Then she founded her own dance school, began to dance and teach, and arrange charity concerts.

In American life, only success and money were respected. Complaining, whining, yearning, or showing negative moods was not accepted. It was the lot of losers. Alena forced herself to seem cheerful, carefree and successful. For better opportunities and a happy future, she helped her daughter and granddaughter move to America. To raise her own self-esteem and improve her self-image, Alena performed plastic surgery. Her good husband tried to support her in everything, traveling the world, taking her on wonderful ocean cruises.

Many years later she again visited Russia. Many people of her generation, who were still alive, sadly eked out a miserable existence with dead eyes, in poverty and abandonment. They no longer hoped for a "happy" future, even for their grandchildren. Alena saw that there was no point for ever returning to her homeland in her declining years. The passions of youth had long abated, and now stability, well-being and peace were the main things for happiness. Accustomed to the comfort, patience and care of her husband, Alena did not see the need to change anything.

Alena clearly knew that material wealth does not make a person happy. Once in her childhood, Alena's grandmother told her: "To be happy, you must try every minute to bring joy to others, and take care of those who are nearby." Happiness is always within man himself. To feel peace of mind, you need to focus on the positive aspects of each day, avoiding disappointment over the little things that are easy to fix. Throwing any negative husk aside, it is important to notice in the person all the best. The law of happiness is to collect particles of joy, string them like beads, and carry a joyful necklace of happiness with you. The Road is Overpowered by the Walking...

***

***

BOOK 1. Coincidences
Part 1. Bright light

During the first nine months of her new life, Alena lay in a very comfortable place, curled up and hiding. It was the most warm, soft and safe place in the world. In addition, this was the only serene, peaceful time of pleasures, when there was no need to think about anything material at all. Sometimes, from somewhere above, wise knowledge and great ideas of the past generations seemed to seep into Alena mind. Then she bounced in amazement, bumping lightly against the soft walls of her first home. Even before she was born, she knew something very important about the world, clearly saw what it was filled with, and why she was going into it. But with each passing month, the space around her became smaller, bringing a sense of anxiety from a closed tightness. Once this feeling of claustrophobia became so unbearable that it was necessary to find a way out. Finally she made up her mind and courageously began to climb forward.

There was a dark and wet tunnel on her way, and a ray of light at the end of it shone, and beckoned with hope, promising joy. After hours of tiring travel, this welcome light finally approached. Alena emerged with her eyes wide open, anticipating happiness. But, suddenly, a short and painful slap met her, instead of a joyful greeting. Along with the "medical slap" in the first second of appearing on this planet, Alena immediately forgot all the wisdom of the past generations. The huge knowledge about the World and the Universe that she received there, behind, in her first house instantly evaporated somewhere. The blow of a hard hand like a magic wand completely erased all the information. But still, for a long time, then there was a strange feeling in her that she knew something enchanting and special. But this well of knowledge seemed was lost forever.

Suddenly Alena found herself in an empty room with a white ceiling and green walls covered with oil paint. From a sharp cold, an unpleasant slap and resentment, and just to, at least, somehow express her disagreement with such an unfriendly greeting, she began to scream loudly, jerking thin legs without muscles and long twisted arms. She called at least someone for help, hoping for care and love. An unsmiling nurse walked in and tightly wrapped the child in a rag, tightly pulling the ends together. The helpless Alena was not able to even lift a finger. She was used to complete freedom in her past comfortable home. It seemed unfair to be held captive by someone else's will. And even more despair swept Alena from this violence and her forced captivity. Unable to do anything, for some time she continued to shout loudly about the lawlessness of the new "arrivals" and the injustice of such treatment. But then she was tired and fell asleep, deciding to find out later all the circumstances and reasons for this not so hospitable meeting.

On the night of Alena's birth, a winter hurricane roared outside the window, drizzled with thorny rain and snow. The strong Northeast wind - Nord-Ost - buzzed in the electro wires, recently appeared in the town, tearing out the new posts and centuries-old trees. On that stormy January night, Alena's uncle, Reanold, tried to get to Gelendzhik, led by his love for his twenty-eight-year-old sister. He wanted to support her in delivering to the Earth such a valuable gift - a new Person. But due to a severe storm, he was stuck at the Novorossiysk railway station, forty kilometers away. No one undertook to steer through the mountains along the steep, winding and narrow road, risking their lives in such darkness and storm. Thus, on this unforgettable, significant night, mother Emma remained in the hospital alone, successfully coping with her difficult, but noble work.

When Alena woke up again, she saw a round ball in front of her nose. A delicious smell emanated from it. But, just in case, Alena turned away in the other direction. What if this is a new trap? But someone stubbornly directed this soft, fragrant ball into her mouth. Alena twisted her head, worried also by the fact that it might not fit inside. And milk splashed into her face. Then this pink ball was still surprisingly easily pushed inside her mouth, and she almost choked on a huge amount of sweet drink. There was so much milk that she was forced to swallow it quickly so as not to choke. However, after a minute she successfully mastered it, and the stream of this warm rain became pleasant and soothing to her. In addition, some very gentle voice whispered: "Sleep my baby, your mother is nearby, and a beautiful world awaits you ahead."

After eating and a lulling voice, Alena felt much better and even a little more confident. She wholeheartedly believed this quiet and loving voice. All these new efforts and excitements plunged her into a long, sound sleep. She dreamed of a joyful and happy life. Her appearance on Earth began with an unexpected slap, but after the first humiliation came the hope and comfort brought by her mother's warm, soothing milk.

So the day passed, and then the second, but no one came to visit them. Alena did not feel anymore the tenderness of her mother, and her caring voice no longer sounded for her. Mom was upset, her milk became bitter. Alena refused to drink it, and cried.

***

Only a few months passed, but Alena acutely felt everything and understood the deep essence of things. It often happened that no one was near her little, painted in lettuce-colored metal crib. There was no one to just shake, talk, or fall in love with a little girl. Even when she wanted to use the toilet, no one came, and lying in her wet and dirty linen was unpleasant. And then, Alena again cried from hopeless despair. Unable to speak and call for the help, she simply screamed because of her helplessness, feeling her loneliness more and more.

In a small resort town on the Black Sea, in the ancient Greek settlement with the strange name Gelendzhik ("White Bride"), a new Guest of the Earth appeared - Alena. On a stormy winter night, her first trip to this planet, her first voyage to life, finally took place. Later, Alena felt that she was very different from the others. In addition, her grandmother, in whose house she was brought up, always emphasized that Alena was a very special girl. All this reinforced her sense of uniqueness. Alena lived as if in a dream, understanding people and animals without words. She was watching what was happening around her, as if from the side. This strange feeling of a "wanderer and an unexpected alien" was always nearby, during all periods of her life. Miraculous transformations came to Alena with her faith in future happiness, and filled her soul with joy. So her miracles in the riddle began. Up down. Believe and wait.

***

Father

Gelendzhik is a city of dreams. People meet in the magical twilight of sunset. The music of the sea breaks into fate, a whirlwind of dance circles, creating new lives. Love lives in the musical passages of the old city. There appeared the life of Alena. The life of her mother, her friends and enemies remained forever there. Fate made a full circle, and once dipped Alena into the fire of unsolved secrets and passions. Once she suddenly found on the Internet old photographs, relics of her heroic grandfather. They had been stolen from his house, and only a bundle of photo paper from the first day of the war, dated June 22, 1941 remained to his relatives. Those photos returned Alena to her childhood, and she began to write her books.

***

Childhood. Amid the hustle and bustle of the day, we have no time to drop by. Only sometimes at night do we open the curtains of memory and wander again in the half-forgotten mazes of painfully bitter or sweet memories of the past. In order to protect a person from too painful memory, nature has created a special protective mechanism, blocking stresses or tragic events of the past. So for a long time Alena did not want to look back into this well of early memory. It was impossible to feel the sharp pain of her childhood losses again. But somehow, on a cruise ship in the Pacific Ocean, multi-colored cubes twisted emotional memory, and suddenly transferred her back to the first months of her life on the Earth. She suddenly remembered a lot of what was hidden behind a heavy curtain.

The future of each child is determined by the way his parents, and especially the mother, treat him in early childhood. When Alena was not even a year old she experienced several heavy emotional blows. Her young mother, Emma, who fought for her honor and independence, was forced to leave her tiny daughter in her grandmother's house, and to go to work in Sakhalin.

Emma was a Russian natural blonde beauty, with beautiful blue eyes looking at the world with the hope of love and fidelity. But from her youth she worked very hard. It never occurred to her to use makeup, do hairstyles, or go for a massage. Alena never saw her caring for herself at all. Therefore, she was very pleased when her mother twice a year, before the big holidays, was dyeing her eyebrows with makeup. Then she looked especially fresh, and at home everyone became joyful.

Emma was the eldest and very obedient daughter. She helped her mother in everything, nursed two younger brothers, and meekly carried the burdens and deprivations of a nomadic life on her shoulders. Her father Minai was military, and by nature cruel and sarcastic. He often laughed at his daughter and criticized her for any oversights. There was no love, no peace, and no comfort in the family. The father figure was damaging for her future. Emma grew up with a dream to meet any strong man who would love her.

Already under the bombing, under the onslaught of the Nazi troops, the family barely escaped from Izhevsk. Shortly after the war, her parents and their many relatives moved to Gelendzhik, to the sleepy little place, far from all troubles. During the war, the military accumulated quite a lot of money. Emma's father, Minai, and his brothers were able to buy quite large pieces of land with a small house. At that time, Emma went to college to study to be an accountant, and re-united with them later.

The stunning resort town by the sea almost year-round was filled by half-naked and very accessible beauties, shamelessly walking along the embankments. They came from all over the Soviet Union not only for recreation, but mainly for new adventures and romance. In a magical town it was impossible to find faithful husbands devoted to their wives. The sea air of the town, saturated with Pitsunda pine, was dizzy to both local residents and vacationers.

The fragrance was especially magnificent in May 1953. The exciting smell of apricot and cherry trees, acacia, lilac and roses drove everyone crazy from awakening passions. In the town, all the men were crazy about the recently arrived beauty Emma. That year, she was often dancing tango in the Primorye Recreation Center, and fell in love with Konstantin Arfanov, the future father of Alena.

Alena's Greek grandfather was also a cheerful handsome man, and was known as a prosperous merchant. He had vineyards near Gelendzik, in Praskoveevka. He often hired assistants to harvest the grapes, and several local families took care of his land and business. But as a result of denunciations by envious persons he, with a group of other successful Greeks, was sentenced to be shot without a trial. He had only one fault was that he was Greek.

The situation of Soviet power after the revolution and the Civil War was precarious. The restoration of the monarchy in Greece in 1935 was also dangerous for the Soviet Union. Among other events of the "Greek" operation, all national Greek schools, publishing houses, and newspapers in the USSR were closed. Other Greeks of the Soviet Black Sea coast were deported to Siberia and the Kazakhstan in freight wagons. Their property was transferred to others in the population. During the "Great Terror" (1937-1938) about 15 thousand Greeks (Soviet and Greek citizens) were arrested.

Stalin (and Yezhov, a Soviet secret police official) signed a Declaration which clearly indicated the number of Greeks who needed to be arrested and how many of them would be shot or sent to camps for 10 years. Only three days were allotted for the preparation of lists with surnames for the issuance of arrest warrants.

***

As recalled the grandmother of Konstantin, Greek Maria, the boy was then only ten years old. He was terribly shocked about the execution and funeral of his father, also Constantine. These tragic events put an indelible mark on both the child and his entire family.

Many years later, trying to find out at least something about the past of her relatives, Alena found on the Internet "Protocol No. 126 of September 5, 1938", where under the number 11 was the name of her Greek grandfather. So, this is how she for the first time suddenly found out about her grandfather: "No. 11. Arfanov Konstantin Georgievich (born in 1906), a citizen of the USSR, place of birth - the village of Praskoveevka, Gelendzhik district, Krasnodar Territory. Sentence - Shoot. "

The mother of little Konstantin, Elena Arfanova, lived near Emma's house. She worked as a teacher in school number 3, where Alena later studied. From the whisper of her relatives, Alena learned that Elena Savvichna was able to convince someone in the registry office to correct several letters in their surname in order to avoid subsequent repressions. As the son of an "executed enemy of the people," the boy Konstantin (like Alena later), grew up surrounded by constant secrets and terrified whispers behind him. This produced a feeling of distrust in him and about everything around him. From childhood, he experienced a sense of fear and anxiety, and new people and a sharp change of scenery were a source of stress. While growing up, Konstantin was not indifferent to spectacular, vibrant women. He was constantly looking for the love and affection that he lacked from childhood.

Konstantin made every effort to attract the attention of the twenty-seven-year-old beauty Emma. They were close in the spring and summer of 1953. Then, Konstantin began strongly to ogle and fool around with other women. He, like other local guys, was looking for entertainment with easily accessible vacationers, and spent most of his time with them. Emma and Konstantin did not get married, as he promised. Emma could not forgive the betrayal of her lover. But the saddest thing was that she could never get rid or forget her bitter past. Konstantin always lived nearby, over the fence, in his comfortable house.

Once, even before the complete break, when Alena was several months old, Konstantin and Emma took a joint photograph. The girl was sitting in her mother's arms. And her father held her hand. All her life Alena remembered her father's striped shirt from that photo. After parting, from the resentment and wanting to erase the painful memory of her first lover, Emma tore his face from all of the few photos that they took together. All her childhood, Alena terribly missed her father and even sometimes saw him in a dream. The first months, Alena and her mother eke out a miserable existence in an old, disheveled shack on the corner of Shevchenko and Sovetskaya, five blocks from Emma's parents' house. This shack with a tiny piece of land Konstantin's grandmother, taking pity on single mother Emma, gave her for very little money.

The shack where Emma lived with her daughter Alena had only one room, a low entrance, and a creaky door. The earthen floor was in some places covered with rotten boards. And on the windows, according to the old custom, wooden sashes hung for security. They could be closed at night only by hand, going outside. Around Emma's house was a small garden. And at the father's fence stood a huge tree, cut half by a shell fragment. The old women said that a bomb fell in the garden when the Nazis bombed the port of Novorossiysk, forty kilometers from Gelendzhik. The house was wrenched from the blast, and it was dangerous to live in. Alena was afraid, listening to the stories about shells that flew near their house and put everyone in mortal danger. And she thought it was lucky that they had not lived there then.

Many years later, Adik, Emma's middle brother, wrote: "With my sister's ex-fiancé, Konstantin, I was always on good terms and met him even after 2000. He then worked in a boarding house "Rainbow" on Pervomaiskaya Street closer to the church. One day, he suggested that I correct my whirls on my head, and I agreed. And after that I often met him walking along the promenade. "

The longing for paternal love and care remained forever in Alena's heart, like an aching wound. Gradually, the subconscious desire to regain father's care turned into a passion for gaining man's loyalty. She took any smallest attention of men or their sexual attraction as love, and often received only suffering and a broken heart.

***

Flood

In 1950th simply trodden paths were near many Gelendzik houses, and later, large stones were laid on them. There was a deep ditch next the walls of Emma's little house. After heavy torrential rains, in November 1954 severe flooding began. Soon water filled and overflowed this ditch. It churned along the paths, and rushed rapidly to the sea in a seething stream. On this day, water completely flooded the earthen floor of Emma's hut. A lot of her simple, poor belongings, and the first photos with her "groom" Konstantin disappeared in that black water. This severe flood also flooded the main street of Lenin near the sea. But the rain kept going and going, and the water rose to the very steps of the hairdresser, where Konstantin worked. Then he remembered his beloved with a child, huddled two blocks from the raging sea.

Seeing that the water is rising, the desperate Emma dressed her daughter in a plush coat and a white knitted hat with bells. She decided to move to her mother, who lived farther to the mountains, on the higher ground. Entering the hut of Emma, Konstantin looked encouragingly at his daughter and his beautiful, kind eyes smiled at her. Alena joyfully extended her hand to him, saying her first word: "Dad!" Father brought with him a

18

rag doll Marfushka. It was single memory about him, and later Alena kept it for a long time.

At that moment, mad Emma screamed loudly in despair that her legs were already "in the muddy streams of mountain's rivers." And then, angrily pointing at Alena, she shouted with anguish: "Here is your daughter, take her and get out of my life." She furiously threw the little girl onto a hard sofa against the wall. Alena's coat slightly softened the impact. But still she felt a sharp pain in the lower part of the spine, and cried from all this unexpected horror. Later, doctors often asked Alena if she had ever had a spinal injury. But the memory for a long time erased from the consciousness of the child all the tragedies and pains of the past. After this terrible scene, ignoring more cries and reproaches from Emma, the miserable Konstantin left, and Alena never saw him again in their house.

***

Abandoned

Hopelessly gritting her teeth, Emma grabbed Alena in her arms, rushed through the horrible storm to her parents. She had nowhere to go. A sharp rain and an evil wind whipped the child in the face. Alena was unhappy and cold. But mother repeated through tears: "Be patient, my little daughter." And Alena believed that her mother still loved her, despite the recent cruel scene. Finally, after running a few blocks, Emma burst into the corridor of her parents. Her mother Anna ran out to meet her. Emma was in frenzy, and sharply threw her daughter in the direction of her mother. She cried out in a torn voice: "I can't live like that anymore!"

For a moment, Alena felt herself somewhere freely falling down. But her grandmother still managed to pick up the girl almost near the floor. Suddenly, Emma's father jumped out of the room, red with anger. He yelled furiously at his unfortunate daughter, insulting and humiliating her: "You dishonored me by messing up with the son of an enemy of the people! Get out of my house!" But his wife Anna answered him, while trying as mush, as she could to protect her poor daughter Emma: "Why? The son is not responsible for the father's unproven fault! "

But Emma's father did not want to listen to them, cursing in disgusting words at the crying Emma. Unable to withstand all the troubles that fell on her, not finding shelter in the parents' house, Emma soon left. When she appeared again she sadly told her mother that she had already bought a ticket to Sakhalin, and would leave in the morning. And so Alena's lonely life began in the house of her good grandmother and her strict grandfather, whom she always feared "like a fire."

Later, father Konstantin tried to establish contact with Alena. But proud Emma always drove him away, depriving her daughter of her father's attention. Later, for some secret family circumstances, Alena received the name of her grandfather and was Filimonov for a while, and was recorded in her grandmother's passport as her own daughter. Alena's surname and patronymic changed several times, fundamentally turning her life around. New names brought new fates.

***

The house of Konstantin and Emma's house stood next to each other. The close proximity of her lover (Alena's father), who betrayed her, was incredibly painful for Emma. Passionate by nature, for a long time Konstantin could not pacify his temper. He had several children with different women, but he continued to sleep around. His official wives, who always lived nearby, scandalized Emma for any reason, jealous of their past love. At times there were disputes about where the border between their tiny gardens was. Often, during the summer nights behind the fence, one could hear Konstantin's fights and battles with his next unhappy wife. Already in his late years in 1970th, one enterprising and judicious woman Valentina was able to finally curb the temperamental Konstantin. She also worked in the same organization as Alena's mother Emma. Later, Alena often saw his two new daughters. They, like all children of Konstantin, were very similar to their father and to each other. His youngest daughter Irina was about the same age as Lila, daughter of Alena. And later they often played together, living in the neighborhood. That's how all the necessary and unnecessary blood ties were intertwined into a tight ball. In Gelendzik almost all old families were relatives among themselves.

***

An excess of trust and generosity also overwhelmed Alena's youth, and her eyes were wide open for good. Then she did not know fear, fear of loss and betrayal. When Alena occasionally looked at her childhood photographs, she saw there a little innocent girl looking at everyone with her big tear-stained eyes, as if asking: "Will you love me?" And she was sad with her.

The first fear comes to a child through the reaction of his mother to surrounding events. The child sees the frightened face of the mother, feels that his mother is afraid of something, and her fear is transmitted to him. Inside Alena, various fears were created by those who lived nearby. Her first and greatest fear came to her at a very early age, when she was no more than two years old. She always remembered the painful picture. Here she weeps in her grandmother's arms, and is struggling to break free. She beats like a wounded bird in the arms of her grandmother and kicks her. Realizing that this should not be happening, she, from terrible powerlessness, pounds with her fists the most beloved person, her grandmother, who is the only one who was always kind and affectionate to her. Alena screams to let her go after her retreating mother, walking away with her suitcases.

But only last night, Alena's mother promised to take her everywhere she would go, promised to take care of her. But then she took out her large suitcase and began to pack her things there. At the same time, Alena's things still were lying down in their places. Alena began to worry, brought her things to her mother, near her suitcase. "Mommy! Please, take me with you! I will help you collect fish on the shore! I will do everything there for you. I will not bother you. Please don't just leave me alone. I feel so bad without you".

Mama promised to take Alena with her, but why were there tears in her eyes. Then mama puts Alena to bed, and quietly, in a breaking voice, sings a lullaby.

***

The next morning Alena woke up too late, and heard an unusual silence in the house. Remembering that last night her mother packed her bags, she immediately shouted with alarm "mother!" But the house answered only with an empty echo. Not hearing the gentle voice of her mother, Alena ran out into the yard. There, her beloved mother had already gone out through the gate into the street. And her mother's brother Rema carried her suitcases. Alena rushed to the gate, screaming in agitation: "You promised to take me with you!" But then grandmother ran up to Alena, grabbed her in her arms and pressed her to her chest. And mother left, not looking back at the heart-rending cries of her daughter.

Alena looked through her burning tears as her mother left, not understanding anything. She only knew that she could not live without her mother. She wanted to run after her, cling to the dress, hug and never part with her. Alena called her for a long time, crying from deep despair. But mother went farther and farther, and was no longer visible. At that moment, Alena's heart was breaking, suffering with fear and unexpected betrayal. Her grandmother was trying to calm, to comfort the child, but her loving words did not help.

This tragic moment of a great shock remained with Alena forever, because emotional memory is the strongest one. Alena's beautiful world of trust and love was destroyed. Grandmother's house was empty, as well as Alena's heart. A cruel lesson of fear, pain and betrayal crashed into the soul of the child. The moment of this sudden separation was like a terrible shock that the girl could never overcome. All her problems of the future came out of many childhood traumas, when she felt abandoned and unloved. This scar was pierced by a deep doubt in the love of loved ones, and the possibility of trusting anyone.

Alena's grandmother, seeing her despair, once said that they had to catch an airplane in order to get to her mother. At that time, on the other side of the bay there was an airport. The airplanes often turned near the grandmother's house, planning for the landing. Sometimes, early in the morning, hoping to fly to her mother, Alena collected her cubes and other simple toys, put them in a small bucket and ran out of the gate. There she stood for a long time and looked up at the sky. Sometimes the plane flew quite low. Alena was sure that the pilot could hear her, and she shouted to her with all her might, her head up to the sky: "Pilot, pilot! Take me to mother in Sakhalin!" But the airplane flew by without landing on the glade near her grandmother's house. Alena's grandfather Minai stood at the gate, looked at her and giggled. Apparently, she was doing something wrong, and she was bitter.

***

For several days Alena thought that her mother would return "soon", as she was promised. Therefore, she took her little bench, stood on it, looking out the window until dark. She did not go to eat or play her favorite games. She just stood there and waited for her mother, feeling that she was very vulnerable, and had absolutely no protection. But in the evening the grandmother approached, and took the girl by the hand: "We should first buy a fur coat, baby; it's always cold in Sakhalin". Grandmother tried to come up with various reassuring stories in order to distract Alena from thinking about her mother, who promised to take her, but who had left alone.

One day in summer, a helicopter landed near the grandmother's house on a meadow, and everyone ran to it. Alena was curious if this helicopter could reach Sakhalin. She, quietly walked next to a woman, got inside, hid under a chair and sat there, until the helicopter took off. And then she got out, sat in the chair, enjoying the view from the window. Then, the Stuart found her: - "Whose are you? Where do you live?" -

And Alena showed them down: "I live down in the garden; my house is the second from the corner! Look, over there my grandmother runs across the field and waves us joyfully. But I need to see my mother on Sakhalin!"

The helicopter made a big circle over the city, and then it was landed back in the meadow. A crying grandmother ran up. She was happy that they found Alena, that at least she had not been stolen as last time. And Alena's grandfather was very angry again. So, when Alena and her grandmother returned home, they sat quietly, embracing, away from her grandfather, reading a book.

Days and weeks passed. So autumn came with its rains. All the time, Alena felt sad, miserable and lonely, as if she lived in a desert. Alena so wanted to see her mother's beautiful face. Every day she continued to stand by the window on the terrace, or in the room by the glass front door. She was afraid to miss mom's return. For her, "soon" meant an hour later; in extreme cases, maybe tomorrow. And once suddenly, it looked like, Alena saw her, so beautiful and so proud, walking around the courtyard in her astrakhan coat, warming her hands in the coupling. Alena was surprised that mom had this old-fashioned, winter clutch, although it was raining outside. Only for some reason mother did not go to the house, but turned to the well, which stood at the neighbor's fence.

- Mother! I'm here! - shouted Alena with all her might.

- Alenochka, my dear, what is wrong with you? - the grandmother's frightened voice came.

- There is mom! My mother is in the yard! I saw her! Open the door faster! Otherwise she went to the neighbors!

Alena beat her slender little bodies in the glass door, calling her mother. But then her stool suddenly turned upside down, and Alena fell down, hit hard on the side of it, and lost consciousness. She remained in this state for a long time. When she regained consciousness she again returned to the glass door, desperately waiting for the promised "soon" return of her mother. She did not want to eat, drink or play for a long time.

Only rubber boots reminded of mom. They were old-fashioned boots with a special recess for the heel. Mom wore them on her beautiful shoes when, in rainy weather, she went to work. Now they lonely clung to the corner on the terrace. Beside them was still standing a navy blue, old convertible stroller. Alena remembered how her mother once pushed her in this stroller somewhere. At that moment, Alena tried to look outside the edge of the raised hood of the stroller to see what was happening around. Any trip to the city from the cramped, dark grandmother's house was a happy adventure for Alena. But her mother raised that hood of the stroller, and it prevented Alena from enjoying the outside world. Alena was upset. At that time, she still could not talk well and just was crying. Her mother was angry with no reason, shouted at her, saying that it was time to sleep. Alena, swallowing tears from an undeserved angry shout, obediently lay at the bottom of the stroller, not wanting to upset her mother. Not finding warmth and tenderness around in the place where she lived, Alena ceased to smile unreasonably and happily.

Winter passed. The pain of loss plunged deeply into the subconscious. Alena tried not to think anymore, and not to ask about her mother. Then spring came with its awakening fragrant nature. And then came her favorite, fun summer, when Alena was finally allowed to go out to play outside. There she spent most of her time hiding from the world among tall flowers or in thickets of fragrant bushes. There she learned a special way to protect herself against offenders. This was taught by a bee. Despite her subsequent death, she deftly took revenge by stinging the attacker.

Most of the year Alena was spending outside, with no control, watch or care by the adults. There she learned how to understand the language of animals and birds, and spoke with them on equal terms. Sitting on warm earth, drowning in the wonderful smell of wildflowers, she spent long hours watching the hard work of the harmonious society of the zealous and defenseless ants. Then she thought that maybe someone out there high above the world of people also follows their actions and can punish the negligent at any moment.

Living without her mother, Alena was for a long time often sick, often fell out of bed, and saw dreams where she was flying. Also, she was a "night walker" - she walked during her sleep without waking up. Her grandmother knew it and watched her, trying to be sure that Alena would not commit something dangerous to her life in her sleep walk. It often happened, when the moon was big, that Alena's grandmother often found her somewhere far in the garden, and gently would talk to her, and bring her back to the house. The first conscious grief of her earlier childhood settled in Alena's soul a deep distrust of people, and of everyone around. All her feelings were aggravated, and she became incredibly suspicious. While watching all people around, she constantly tried to understand what they think and how they relate to her. It was during this period that she began to deeply doubt that someone really loved her. Alena's attitude to others and her own behavior depended on what Alena thought and felt about people.

From early childhood, two terrible beasts settled in her heart: loneliness and separation. It seemed that only they alone belonged to her completely, and were the only ones who did not betray. Life around her was full of contradictions and secrets, and little Alena fought alone with her inner demons. Every day was filled with various fears. She often took conscious and unconscious risk with one desire: to excel. She needed to stand out, to overcome something, to be ahead of everyone, to be better than everyone, so that only she would finally be noticed and respected. Often, fighting for the opportunity to feel the care of loved ones, and fearing them, Alena tried to defend herself by simply smiling at everything that was happening or hiding silently. She realized very early that even the closest people inflicted mental pain and she tried to avoid them. More and more rejecting the outside world, she closed herself in, not trusting anyone, but still expecting some kind of miracle.

After the tragedies of childhood and too early mental trauma, Alena experienced several complexes. One of them was the fear of being late somewhere. It came to her that one morning when her mother left home while Alena was still sleeping. This strong fear of "not being late" lived forever inside her. It was so old and so strong that even when Alena was delayed for only one or two minutes, she already felt unpleasant stress. Therefore, she tried to come everywhere in advance. Later analyzing the events of distant childhood, Alena unraveled their roots.

***

Relatives

Greek great-grandmother Maria lived only one block from Emma's house and two blocks from Grandmother Anna's house. She seemed a very old, dark and dried up woman. Only her big, black eyes were very alive and shined with a very strong light. One might have felt that her eyes could burn you alive, if she only wished it. Anyway, she moved slowly, helping herself with a crutch, and looked like a sorceress from the fairy tale Sleeping Beauty.

Despite her strange appearance, she was very kind to Alena, and the girl felt that the old-old great-grandmother Maria really loved her. When they passed by her house, she tried to pat Alena on the head with her thin, bony hand, and often secretly shoved candy or even money into Alena's pocket. Alena thought that she was purposefully sitting there, on her corner with one goal - to meet Alena. Great-grandmother Maria often whispered meaningfully in Alena's ears: "Don't worry about anything. I passed you a very special gift. You have a very bright future, and always will get whatever you want. Your beauty is a powerful force. Use that gift carefully; do not waste it in vain. And I will always protect you, my beautiful child."

Then, they talked for a while with Alena's Russian grandmother. After that, all the way to Emma's house, grandmother Anna was silent and looked very serious, like she learned some mystical wisdom, closed to her before that. Unfortunately, with each year, Alena's mother and grandmother tried to prevent Alena from communicating with her Greek relatives. But in a small town it was impossible to hide something. Gradually Alena became acquainted with her Greek relatives, and dreamed that they openly recognized her as their own. The Greeks often met her on the streets, talked about their ancient family, and about other members of the huge clan. In Alena's heart they created the feeling that she should be proud of her ancient Greek roots, which originated in the family of King Constantine. Especially kind was her father's sister, Olga, who lived nearby. It was her aunt Olga who brought up a spirit of pride in Alena for her own beauty and self-esteem. She helped her to believe in her own strengths and overcome the problems of "abandonment" and alienation Alena always felt while growing up.

Only in the summer it was relatively good to be living in the poor and small house of her Russian grandmother. Her grandmother Anna was very hospitable. So, every summer many relatives came to her to relax by the sea without paying her anything. Alena rejoiced at people who had nothing to hide from her. To Alena's questions about her father, they answered her that he was a long-distance sailor. She believed this and was waiting for him. For street walks, Alena was often dressed up in a beautiful marine suit. She was very proud of it, thinking that this outfit was sent to her by a loving father, and this brought them together. In the port area, there were a lot of sailors walking in the evenings, wearing flared trousers. Alena's height was to their knees, and while walking with her mother along the street, she grabbed the bottom of their wide trousers. And then, with her head up, she asked: "Have you met my father?" But the sailors only smiled back and passed by. Once one of them crouched and affectionately asked her name, gaily glancing at the beautiful mother. For Alena, this attention was like a victory. She was convinced that the sailor stopped nearby only for her own sake. Then she thought: "Or maybe he is my dad?"

Grandmother Anna told her daughter Emma that the pride and s love to a man fight inside the souls of a woman. She was very angry with the reckless choice of her daughter Emma, and with her choice to be with Alena's father Konstantin. Also, she was angry with her own husband Mina, who had several illegitimate children in Gelendzhik. Generally, grandmother often spoke negatively about all men of the world, probably for Alena's educational purposes. Or maybe she just wanted to share her sorrows with at least someone, and only the little granddaughter was her silent listener. Grandmother Anna, raising Alena, did not particularly think that her negative grunts would shape the girl's life. Alena absorbed her grandmother's character and views. She grew up with a hostile attitude towards men, believing, following her grandmother, that all men are second-class people who can do nothing but children, and therefore do not deserve much respect.

For several years, mother Emma lived and worked in Sakhalin. She rented a room at her uncle Ivan Pugachev (Filimonov). He also once had a fight with his brother Minai on the political issues, and left Gelendzhik forever. Only a few years later, when Alena had almost forgotten her mother, she suddenly returned. But communication and trust were undermined, and she seemed to Alena completely alien. In addition, her mother brought with her a young stepfather Gregory, who immediately disliked an independent and proud girl.

In the early 1960s, having received permission from the city authorities, mother and stepfather began to build a large house on the spot where Emma's old shack was once. They were completely absorbed in building that house, and in their lives, rarely paying attention to a seven-year-old girl. Alena, as before, was left to herself. Over time, Emma's new home, conveniently located in a wonderful place, two blocks from the sea, began to arouse envy. Many people desired to take possession of it. So there were new problems that captured Emma, and in the fight against them, her daughter was again in the last place.

***

***

Pearls

The whirlwinds of fate, like the waves of a raging ocean, took off and fell, dragging a person along, and continuing to weave their invisible, connecting threads.

One day in the early 2000s, Alena and her American husband Victor were on a comfortable cruise ship. In general, they traveled a lot together, especially in the first ten years of their surprisingly harmonious and happy life. Once, their huge, sixteen-story ocean liner had been hanging out in the South Pacific for more than a week. In this foggy water expanse without borders, strange sensations and thoughts visited Alena. But there was a lot of entertainment on the ship, so there was no time to yearn or be bored. Every day they went to concerts and various lectures. Alena was especially interested in hearing about pearls. It was said that the main characteristic of pearls is that they don't overshadow their owner, but only emphasizes her natural attractiveness and femininity. It is no accident that pearls have always been a symbol of purity, innocence and restraint. The frames of icons, church vestments, altars and bindings of the Bibles were decorated with pearls. Also, for some mysterious reason, pearls have always had a strong influence on Alena.

Finally, the huge liner reached one of the small islands of the Pacific Ocean called Bora Bora. Walking along the shore, they saw sellers of pearls, and bought some beautiful strands of white and black pearls. Returning to the ship, Alena did not part with the beads. She fingered them, like a rosary, stroked and felt that something incredibly familiar was blowing from them. For that foggy night in the Pacific Ocean, Alena for some reason could not sleep.

The ocean has always had a strange, even mysterious influence on Alena. And suddenly, in the quiet night of the vast ocean, the tightly-closed draperies of her childhood memory rose, and she remembered why she was so attracted to pearls. She finally found the courage to look behind the black wings of a deep veil. A shocking discovery occurred in the Pacific Ocean. Alena clearly saw her mother, again standing in front of her in her favorite pearls. She suddenly remembered the secret of her mother's priceless pearl beads. Then only did Alena realize what kind precious jewelry she had lost.

***

For many years, in a closet of the Leningrad apartment, Alena kept amazing, completely round, heavy, white pearls. Each pearl was about sixteen millimeters in diameter. Between the pearls were solid wax nodules that separate and protect them from colliding with each other. However, this long string of pearls was torn in several places and wrapped in an old handkerchief. They were special pearls, grown for many decades and mysteriously glowing from the inside. It was impossible to take your eyes off of them. Alena's grandmother called them "Pearls of Mikimoto." The incredibly beautiful necklace of rare pearls was a real masterpiece that Alena did not even suspect. It was a sad memory for her about her mother who had left so early.

Once, in the Pacific Ocean, a shocking discovery occurred. Alena suddenly remembered the secret of priceless pearl beads. Then only did Alena realize what kind of jewelry she had lost. She could not sleep that night on the American ship. She saw that some of these beautiful beads still seemed to be next to her, the little girl Alena. They crashed into her memory with a sorrowful symbol of a lost treasure, a symbol of broken love and unfulfilled happiness. A painful childhood memory wounded her soul with the acuteness of heavy losses, and shed tears on her pillow in their comfortable luxury cabin.

***

In one of her old albums, Alena stored a very old photograph from 1959. In this photo, she recalled her incredibly beautiful mother, who so much hoped for happiness, smiled slightly, as sad as a smile of Giaconda. The photograph was supposed to symbolize the beginning of a new family, which, after many years of separation, Emma planned to create by bringing a "new dad" for Alena from Sakhalin Island. But the deeply wounded daughter, who for a long time had been waiting for her mother, was jealous of her stranger. And when she came back, she still disappeared to somewhere or spent time with her new husband. All of Alena's hopes for her mother's care and attention were in vain.

On that day going to take a memorable photo, everyone dressed up. Photography in general was a big event for people at that time. For this occasion, mother specially wore precious beads made of stunning white pearls. These beads were so long that she wrapped them around her neck twice, and then, she tied them into a small spectacular knot.

Either because mother was in a hurry, or because she did not know how to do it before, Emma quickly poked her daughter's beautiful hair with a sharp comb, and stuck a white bow on her head. Then Alena began to be forced to wear a new, "crepe de Chine" dress, which her stepfather chose for her. But this dress was shamefully transparent, unpleasantly prickly and simply shapeless. Alena had an innate craving for beauty, and her grandmother instilled in her a taste for simple, comfortable things. The girl immediately disliked this indefinite color outfit and did not want to wear it. But her mother forced her to do this contrary to the wishes of the child, not reckoning with the feelings of her daughter, but only to please her new husband. Alena hopelessly obeyed, crying with despair. And then, all the way to the city Alena was very upset. In the photo shop she wouldn't want to stand next to this stranger and smile to him.

From the day one, the stepfather immediately began to smugly and rudely bring her up. And then, on this solemn day, which was supposed to be a celebration for everyone, he began to "lecture" and teach Alena's mother, loudly expressing his dissatisfaction with the girl's behavior. The good mood was spoiled. Alena saw that her beloved mother was very upset by his negative nit-picking and disagreement with her daughter. But most of all, Alena was outraged by the behavior of this man, stinking of beer. Although, he was younger than her mother, he dared to dictate what she should do with her own child.

A rude, narrow-minded person who had just burst into their lives caused her rejection. Alena considered him an empty place, and was sure that he had no right to scold her. A five-year-old girl was defenseless, but she deeply understood everything around her. At that moment, when he spoiled her joy for taking photo with her mother, she was swallowing the bitter tears of disrespect for her personality. She answered him rudely, but while glancing at her mother for help. She was looking for mother's protection. Alena could not believe that her mother would choose a stranger instead of her child. It was the same terrible betrayal that Alena had already experienced from her once before. A few years ago, mother broke her promise, and left her, going to this Gregory. From that moment, Alena hated that Gregory forever.

A 1959 photograph forever captured the stepfather's angry, evil face and sad mother, still hopefully trying to smile. Alena stood there, offended, with tears in her eyes. She did not want to hug anyone, uncomfortably and tightly sandwiched between two adults who dreamed of their own happiness. There was no place for an illegitimate child who was always a reproach and a reminder of the mistakes of youth.

***

Soon, mother disappeared again. Once again, as always, Alena played alone in her grandmother's house. She often came into this "cold" room and stayed there for hours. She enjoyed opening the drawers, and examining her mother's things that were stored there. When the longing for her mother especially greatly angered her soul, Alena even looked inside a small old closet. Almost all the things in the closet smelled like mothballs. But her mother's few dresses smelled of her favorite perfume "Red Moscow". For the girl it was like the smell of her mother. She loved to caress and feel these dresses with the smell of her mother. At such moments, it seemed to her that her mother was nearby, did not leave anywhere at all, and did not miss so many events of her childhood.

Once Alena could not resist and, despite all her grandmother's terrifying prohibitions, she took out from the closet her mother's favorite necklace. For Alena, these pearls were magical. She heard that these beads were sacredly kept under lock and key because they were a gift from her Greek father. This fact reinforced for Alena the significance and value of the necklace. Alena quietly played with pearls, sitting on the couch, stroking and kissing beads. Although she felt that she was doing something forbidden, she still could not stop. She admired this precious memory of her mother. Suddenly, grandmother entered the room. Alena realized that she was caught red-handed, and, frightened, immediately hid the necklace behind her, quickly pushing it under the pillow. And grandmother, in a fright, screamed angrily at her, grabbed the beads and began to pull them to herself. Alena was indignant at the harshness of her usually loving and affectionate grandmother. She held the beads tightly, and also shouted: "No, I won't give it to you! These are my mother's beads. I have the right to just touch them."

34

They pulled the string of beads in different directions, and no one wanted to concede. And suddenly the priceless necklace exploded. Snow-white, perfectly round, one to one, with a loud bang, pearls were falling on the bare wooden floor. Heavy balls of pearls pounded hopelessly and tragically, like Alena's heart, and rolled under the sofa. Grandmother and Alena sobbed at the same time, each on her own occasion. One cried bitterly from torn beauty and the other from her ruined life. And suddenly, out of nowhere, Alena's mother ran into the room into the noise. Seeing what happened, her face changed and darkened. But she did not say anything, did not swear. But she did not try to comfort the child, either. Grandmother whispered timidly through tears:

-"Maybe we could take them to a jewelry workshop and fix it?"

-"No. They would be stolen."- said mother

Some of these beautiful beads still lay next to Alena. They crashed into her memory a woeful symbol of a lost treasure, a symbol of broken love and unfulfilled happiness.

***

Once in 1994, before leaving Russia, Alena decided to fix her mother's pearl string. She took them to a jewelry store in Leningrad. The receptionist behind the window, glancing quickly at the beads, immediately went into the other room, hidden by the curtains. Soon an old, fat and unpleasant store owner came out. When he saw the old pearl beads, his hands began to tremble. But Alena did not pay special attention to this. He spoke irritably to her, demandingly asking where she had taken these beads. Alena suddenly, as in childhood, was frightened by his unreasonably rude voice, so similar to the evil voice of her stern grandfather, punishing her for all the wrongdoings. Alena quietly replied to the Jew jeweler: "My mother died. And now it remains ..."

After a pause, and not releasing the precious pearls from his thick, sweaty fingers, the jeweler barked that he would collect the pearls with a new thread, replacing the broken one. "Come back in a week," he snapped rudely, and somehow strangely began to put Alena on the street. Alena left this store with a heavy feeling. She could not find peace and could not sleep, thinking that she had done something irreparable. She returned to this jewelry store a few days later and was immediately given the same length of white "pearl". She was very surprised at his lightness, and said that this was not what she left with them. But the woman in the window began to resent and hiss at Alena, claiming that everything was right. "Take what you got and get out," she muttered roughly, but firmly.

Rudeness and insults always shocked Alena. If someone insulted her or showed her cruelty, she was always very lost and stiff. So it was this time. Alena realized with horror that the jeweler, as her mother had warned many years ago, replaced precious pearls with white plastic balls. At that terrible moment of this stunning discovery, Alena with terrible fear realized that she had been robbed. The rare pearls of her mother were taken away. But most importantly, they robbed her from the only precious memory of her mother.

Alena's grandmother carefully preserved these priceless pearls for many decades after the early death of her daughter Emma. A beautiful necklace kept many memories. It was a symbol of Alena's mother's first love. It was a memory of Alena's waiting, and the symbol of her hope. For a long time, Alena with her own daughter Lila was starving, suffering and living in poverty. At the same time, a treasure wrapped in a simple, old handkerchief was kept in her Leningrad apartment. No one ever suspected its real value. Then, the pearl beads so irrevocably were gone forever.

***

Probably due to the deep wounds of her childhood, Alena was always deeply focused on her feelings and emotions, constantly delving into her experiences. Living deep inside herself, she seemed to live life in "pink glasses", looking at everything, as if from the outside, as a spectator.

Many years have passed since this last tragic case of Russian life. And then one day in the Pacific Ocean, Alena's kind husband bought her a gift, a beautiful string of white pearls. When Alena saw its true price, she was enormously surprised and gasped. Her memory, which had kept the pain of childhood grievances for so long, suddenly returned to her, burning with the bitterness of her lost pearls. Alena infinitely regretted that throughout her life in Russia she was so blind and knew so little real life. It was a severe shock that struck her in the Pacific Ocean.

The ocean was still the same. He also washed the shores of the distant island of Sakhalin, where once her mother escaped from adversity. Emma lived and worked for a long time off the Pacific coast. And in Gelendzhik she was awaited by delightful pearls, a generous symbol of her first love. This ocean knew the hands and love of her mother. And this ocean once returned to Alena the indelible pain of irreparable, deepest loss. But the past is always too late and useless to regret. Everything disappeared, everyone left, disappeared forever. Life repeated the only wisdom: if there is love, it must be protected. We must love and protect those who are near. But people do not learn this lesson. Alena also could not teach this to those whom she loved more than anything.

***

Память о курорте
Геленджикъ 1961.

Binding Threads

In mid-August 1961, Alena stood at the low window of her grandmother's house, and listened to the radio. She looked sadly into the garden, saying goodbye to her childhood. Anxious thoughts flashed through the girl's head. This August, there were big changes in her life. It was a turning point in her life.

It was the last carefree summer in the house of her beloved grandmother Anna, where she lived from birth. Recently, her mother with a new husband returned to Gelendzhik. In place of Emma's old shack, they built a large, beautiful house. Soon Alena was supposed to move into it to live there. But this was not good news for Alena. She hated the unpleasant, bad smelled, thin-lipped stepfather. From the first days he "exercised" his rights, and sharply indicating to Alena's mother how she should deal with her daughter. In the conflicts and in the disputes with Alena, his mother treacherously took the side of her new husband, trying to please him in everything. Alena could not forgive mother for that betrayal.

Sometimes, for show, expressing his "care", her step father took the child Alena to his lap and whispered some compliments. But this was extremely unpleasant, because soon under Alena something swelled getting bigger. It was a shame to sit on his lap, and Alena fled in a panic. Her relatives were surprised at her bad manners, called her "wild", and no one listened to the little girl's arguments. Despite her stubborn resistance, in the new conditions Alena had to follow what was decided without her participation.

In this autumn another significant event was coming. In September, Alena was going to go to her first grade of school. But this event did not look good either for the freedom-loving girl. She heard from her friends on the street that the teachers were strict, controlling everything in the school, asking all sorts of lessons. In addition, they will force her to do everything that Alena did not like to do at all. These disturbing thoughts flashed through the head of a girl standing by the window.

Suddenly the announcer indignantly announced the shocking news. Twenty-year-old American student Victusha and his friend tried to hide a girl in the trunk of their car in order to transport her from East Berlin to West. But they were stopped, searched and sent to prison. The boy's grandmother named Emma, as all his relatives, was terribly worried and tried to help him.

Coincidentally, she had the same name as Alena's mother, which surprised Alena. She was sure, that only her mother could have such a rear name as Emma. At the same time, while listening to Soviet radio, hysterically condemning American students, Alena could not imagine that in some magical way, thirty-five years later, this boy Victusha would become her devoted and loving husband. Verily, the ways of the Lord are mysterious. Invisible, binding threads rushed to the other end of the earth, across the ocean, continued to weave the paths of fate and connect the future with the present.

Some years later, in the other summer, Alena walked with the girls who rented a room in her mother's house. They chatted merrily, not paying any attention to the teenager, and had fun with the famous game of "cities". The most difficult thing was that each new city had to start with the same letter that the name of the previous city ended with. But soon their knowledge of the cities ran out, and the game stopped. Then they began to express their cherished dreams aloud, boasting about those amazing places where each of them would like to live. One girl arrogantly said that she would live "only in the capital of our country." And everyone looked at her with envy, because she dreamed of something incredible, like from a fairy tale.

At that time, many residents of the province dreamed of living in the more prosperous and exciting Moscow. But it was almost impossible. However, her mother's younger brother Reanold already lived in Moscow, and also two grandmothers' brothers lived there. After the Second World War (1941-1945), her grandmother for a long time searched for her relatives, and she found them ten years later in Moscow. In winter, leaving from the cruelty of her unfaithful husband, she took Alena to visit her relatives. So, Alena knew what Moscow was about. She had no desire to live there, in a cold, noisy, fussy and huge city. But to express her knowledge of Moscow aloud to the fussy girls would be foolish. Nevertheless, Alena wanted to quickly announce something unusual, so that they would pay attention to her and show some respect. Then, Alena loudly and firmly declared: "And I will live in America!"

In the 1960s, during the outbreak of the Cold War with America, to wish such strange thing and in a loud voice was simply outrageous revolutionary blasphemy. So, everyone just maliciously laughed at such an awkward, wild joke, continuing on their way, and not looking anymore at the daring girl. If they had only known that the Lord heard these words, and fulfilled everything. Many years later it happened.

In the meantime, to sensitive and sharp-eyed Alena, her own life continued to bring many downs and ups, joys and tragedies. Invisible, connecting threads continued to weave the paths of fate and to connect the future with the present. The whirlwinds of fate, like the waves of a raging ocean, took off and fell, dragging a person along, and continuing to weave their invisible, connecting threads.

The whirlwinds of fate, like the waves of a raging ocean, took off and fell, dragging a person along, and continuing to weave their invisible, connecting threads. And then, when Alena was also only twenty years old, she experienced a situation similar to Victusha, when he was only twenty. For a short time, but she ended up in a Soviet prison, so similar to the Berlin prison.

***

Berlin Prison

After the defeat of fascist Germany, the territory of Berlin was divided into two zones. The eastern part was under the influence of the USSR. The western part of Berlin was under the United States, Britain and France. At first, the border between the western and eastern parts of Berlin was open, and thousands of people crossed it daily. They could compare living conditions of two parts of Berlin. In August 1960, West Germany refused a trade agreement with the eastern part of the country. East Germany was regarded it as an "economic war." On August 13, 1961, the Berlin Wall was built there, which lasted until 1989. This happened just two weeks before the trip by Victusha and his fellow countryman Gilb to Berlin. Prior to this, Victusha attended a summer school in Oslo, and his friend studied in France. Gilb learned that Victusha had a fashionable Volkswagen car, and suggested meeting him in Berlin during the summer vacation and going on a trip around Germany. Although the world was in a difficult political situation, American tourists could easily cross the border between East and West Berlin. Their passports were checked, but the car was usually not searched. At that time, Volkswagen was one of the most popular cars in Germany, and it was called a "People's Car". The car was painted it mainly in all shades of blue or red. Defiantly red Volkswagen was very popular in America. One of the agricultural organizations, with which father of Victusha collaborated, offered to buy this quality machine for them. They asked Victusha to buy the red Volkswagen and send it to America across the ocean.

In East Berlin the public telephones were cheap, and one day, the guys decided to call home in California. At the post office, the employee demanded a special document confirming on what grounds the students own the currency, and where they received it from. From an unexpected obstacle and the injustice of the demand, the quick-tempered Gilbert entered into a rather sharp argument with the clerk. But the clerk did not understand English well, and the guys did not know German. But then suddenly a

German student Erica hastened to their aid. She stood in the line behind them, and volunteered to be their translator. But the clerk was already furious with the behavior of "arrogant American snobs." The guys did not have a document for currency, and they could not call home. Gilb and Victusha left the post office and the girl immediately left after them. After they left, the mail clerk most likely immediately called the security service, telling about the incident.

Leaving the post office, the guys were very upset and vigorously discussed the incident. With keen sympathy for them, Erica offered to act as their guide, and show new friends areas of East Berlin that had not yet been completely restored after the war. Having talked, she complained about the construction of a wall that separated her family and her lover. Knowing that she was very at risk, the fragile girl still tried to put pressure on the guys' pity, taking advantage of their inexperience. She even managed to confuse their head with a story that she plans to escape to the Western part of Berlin in a tourist bus. It seemed even to the romantic American students quite implausible. They began to politely admonish her so that she would not do such stupidity. Then she, as if casually, hinted that this could be done in the trunk of their car.

Cautious Victusha at first flatly refused. Given the international tension and the outbreak of the Cold War, young Victusha strongly doubted the reasonableness of what the energetic adventurer Gilb suggested he do. Grieving, Erica nevertheless asked to send at least a letter to her relatives in the forbidden part of the city. Although this was also illegal, but Victusha, reluctantly agreed, yielding to the onslaught of his two opponents.

The next day, the guys, having delivered the letter and safely returned to the communist Eastern part of the city, met with Erica. Then she again, word for word, began to convince them to transport her to the other side. Doubts about the rationality of such a rash act greatly tormented Victusha's soul. And he quietly said that the trunk is very small, and she will not fit there. But the stubborn Gilb puffed up and ranted, wanting to show himself a hero, convincing Victusha that it was safe and easy to do. In the end, Victusha, by his natural gentleness, yielded to persuasion. Erica, for security reasons, suggested meeting at night on a quiet street to hide in the trunk without prying eyes. Although the trunk was tiny, the fragile girl somehow, with joy, fit in there.

In East Berlin crammed with spies. It looked, like even the houses had eyes and ears. They began their journey across the border at about ten in the night. This clearly seemed suspicious to the border guard, and was another irreparable mistake. When students arrived at a checkpoint in a red Volkswagen, they were immediately stopped. The border guards asked them to open the trunk and found Erica there. The irreparable happened. East German soldiers arrested them, sent to a prison, and the car was confiscated. Young Americans were brought into the common room, where they met with two Sudanese students, British and Dutch merchants, who were caught for about the same "crime". Officials interrogated everyone and sentenced to two years in prison. Victusha regretted about his participation in that event all his life. Newspapers of many countries were full of headlines: "German Reds imprison two American students" and "Red sentence to 2 American youths for escape". And communist propaganda shouted condemningly about "the shame of American spies."

Only after some time, Victusha's father suddenly found out about the arrest of his son. A dumbfounded neighbor called him in horror, and said that something completely unbelievable had happened with his son Victusha. At that time, most Americans were busy with their peaceful lives distant from European problems. So Victusha's family had the most "superficial" idea of the strange wall dividing Berlin. They were simply terribly frightened by the unprecedented cruelty of the verdict for their so obedient son, accustomed to living by the rules. Desiring to immediately release him, his father began to look for all sorts of ways to do this. He talked with different people who had at least some influence in East Germany. Then, he flew to Berlin several times. At the same time, Victusha's father understood the senselessness of seeking help from the US government. At that time, the United States had not yet recognized the Eastern Germany government. "If we had a US representative there, they would very quickly release my son," - his father later said.

Help came from the influential Sunkist Growers organization, with which Victusha's father had long, close contacts, selling his oranges through them. The Sunkist distribution center was both in West Germany and in France. One of the officials of this organization exchanged West German goods for East German goods, and knew someone in the government of East Germany. Also, this man Brans found a German lawyer for the arrested guys because the East German government did not recognize the American family lawyer for Victusha's defense.

A lawyer from East Berlin spent a week with his Victusha's father, helping him to write a letter to the head of Communist government of East Germany. This letter was to be written only in German, emphasizing respect for the nation (as the lawyer emphasize). Although for Victusha's father, a true American from head to toe, it was incredibly difficult to do, the letter was written in such a way as to cajole and flatter Walter Ulbricht. The letter said that two romantic boys, not understanding the seriousness of the crime, simply out of nobleness, made a mistake. And that American people hope that "the great father of the German Republic will forgive the guys for what they did and set them free."

But Ulbricht decided to use American students as an example to show the world that the new socialist government of East Germany cannot be played the fool. Only after four months, with great difficulty, it became possible to release Victusha and Gilb from the German prison. They stayed there longer than Sudanese students and traders from other countries.

The first, most terrible month, Victusha spent there, in a solitary, concrete cell. Its width was equal to his open arms, and it was about 10 feet long. The toilet was a bucket (barrel) in the corner. Victusha slept on a rotten, worn, thatched mattress, which was thrown onto a slightly raised, concrete platform. Sometimes he managed to get some nonsense book, a German textbook and a bible. Only once a week the guards let him out into the narrow courtyard for a walk, and sometimes giving him a shovel for work. A shovel for Victusha was a familiar tool, and he perceived this obligation rather as entertainment, and happily worked. In the silence of the solitary confinement, Victusha continued to convince himself that it would all be over soon. It never crossed his mind that in reality, everything was much more serious than he had supposed. In 1986, he recalled: "I lost a lot of weight. My teeth hurt from hard bread and sausages. Once we were given several slices of tomato and onion. It seemed to me an incredible delicacy, and I asked for more. But they refused me."

Relatives were allowed to visit their twenty-year-old, exhausted son only after a month of his imprisonment. "He looked like a corpse, it was just awful to look at him," his father recalled. After a month of being in a solitary hole, his father managed to have Victusha transferred to a common cell with six people. The spacious chamber had more acceptable conditions for existence. But its main advantage was the luxury of human communication.

Once, while walking through the prison, Victusha caught a glimpse of Erica. But she walked far down the corridor and did not notice him. Four months later, when Victusha and Gilb were ordered to change clothes for release, in the prison closet they saw the same coat of Erica which she wore on the day of her arrest. She was still in prison. Her punishment was harsher; there was no one to intercede for her.

These tragic events in a German prison shocked Victusha a lot. Shame and guilt haunted him for a long time. Most likely, therefore, a sensitive and sentimental man, Victusha married early, passionately seeking solace, love and understanding. But it was his naive mistake of youth, as he recalled many years later. Returning from Germany, Victusha forever blocked the memory of those terrible events of his youth, not wanting to remember or talk about his suffering. These sad events of his youth did not allow him to feel like a big hero, as the American press wanted to describe. Once, he finally gave an interview about his painful time in prison. Explaining his behavior in Germany, already a forty-five-year-old, highly respected person, the director of several organizations, Victusha said: "I have been asked many times if I would do it again. That would depend on my knowledge of the consequences. I don't know how to put it, not sounding like a "super patriot". But there was someone who suffered in the framework of the system that we considered unfair. We had the opportunity for direct intervention. And we did it. "

Victusha's friends, speaking of his character, emphasized that without hesitation he always upheld what he considered to be right. One of his friend, a citrus producer, Rick once emphasized that "Victusha is a first-class guy." Continuing the work of his great-grandfather, grandfather and father, Victusha was engaged in agriculture since childhood, growing oranges and avocados. He traveled a lot around the world, sharing his experience and knowledge. East German officials invited him to their country, but Victusha did not have the slightest desire to visit them.

***

In August 1961 such events took place with American guy Victusha. At the same time, seven-year-old Alena stood at the window of her grandmother's house, listening to the radio about his sad adventure in Berlin. Already long ago, invisible threads of fate stretched across the Pacific Ocean and connected them with each other. But they still did not know this at all. Each of them will live own life, with all its ups and downs. They will walk towards each other a long way, and finally, one day, they will happily unite.

Arrest

During long time anybody could get into the Russian prison with no proven fault. This is why there was a proverb "don't announce that you would not be in the prison or would not be a beggar". This could happen to anybody at any time. The whirlwinds of fate, like the waves of a raging ocean, took off and fell, carrying the man along with him. They continued to weave their invisible, connecting threads between Alena and Victusha, between the present and the future. When Alena was also only twenty years old, she also experienced a situation similar to Victusha.

***

Alena grew up a naughty, extremely incredulous and suspicious and very impressionable child. Due to the circumstances of her birth and the situation of her family, the girl from an early age lived in an atmosphere of secrecy and confusion. But she had a deep instinct, intuition, and did not tolerate any secrets around her. When she felt that something was hiding from her, then by all means, she tried to solve it and did not stop until all secret became clear. This often led her into much trouble. But she could not do anything about it, keenly and skeptically perceiving the world, and did not trust anyone. Later, the cold attitude of her family was aggravated by her hated stepfather, making her life in mother's house simply unbearable. Having no close relationship with her mother, Alena spent time reading books, twisted in the illusions of a fictional world, dreaming of faithful love. Alena did not want to obey anyone, living by her own rules. With her mother, who abandoned her in her childhood, she often quarreled terribly for any reason, especially because of the tricks of her alcoholic stepfather. He hated Alena, especially after the birth of his own son, and tried his best to oust her from her home.

In the last grade of school, Alena, rather due to pity and curiosity, began dating her lame classmate. Knowing nothing about sex, shortly after prom she discovered her pregnancy. She was only seventeen years old, when under the pressure of public opinion Alena was forced to marry, as they say, "at gunpoint." The family told her that "the child must have an official father" so that she would not be considered "disgraced" in society. But her first marriage was a mistake, and soon turned into many betrayals. This unfortunate marriage exacerbated her already huge problem of trust in people.

After registering the marriage, her young husband Sergey continued to live with his parents, and brought them his salary. Alena with the daughter Lila lived in her mother's house and survived alone as she could. Her husband rarely visited them, did not try to see his daughter or help them with anything. A year later, Sergey's parents sent him to the University of Novosibirsk. Finally, he got his complete freedom; Sergey was happy to live as free as he wanted or was good for him, drank a lot and slept around. Knowing nothing about this, the naive Alena made attempts to "save the family". She flew to him several times, tried to adapt to the fierce cold of the Siberian town. She suffered for a long time the bullying of her drug addict husband, and did not have any chance or money to get out of there, or somehow ending her too early, difficult marriage. Only two years later, having sold all her personal belongings, she returned to Gelendzhik. The first marriage of Alena, as one would expect, was a mistake, and soon turned into a lot of betrayals. This miserable marriage exacerbated her already huge problem of trust in men.

***

In the summer of 1974 first Alena's husband, former classmate Sergey came to Gelendzhik for a vacation. He visited Alena's house and had a fight with her uncle. Outraged Alena wanted to avenge her crippled husband. She wrote an insulting letter to the work of her relative in Moscow. Her uncle's career was in jeopardy, and he started a trial against Alena. But Alena did not expect that her uncle would take her to a court to restore his reputation. At that time, she was quarreling with her relatives, and moved with her daughter to live in a three-room apartment of her mother-in-law. But her mother-in-law was not happy with new tenants, and turned Alena's life into another nightmare.

Alena tried to continue her education at the Krasnodar University, and soon needed to go there for exams. Then, she thought that maybe her first husband would like to restore their marriage. So, she bought tickets to go to him in Novosibirsk again. One morning, Alena took her daughter to a kindergarten, and then went to her work. She told her boss, that she will quit the job, and needed to get her money. But suddenly three men in black suits silently approached her. They took her by the arms, put her in a car, and took her to prison.

Alena begged to give her the opportunity to call home and bring her more comfortable clothes. And most importantly, she needed to get her daughter from the kindergarten. Only at the end of the day, finally, the police on duty, taking pity on her pleas and looking around the empty corridor, gave her the phone. Sergey's mother was not distinguished by sensitivity or kindness. Stubborn mother-in-law could not understand anything from Alena's confused explanation. She began to yell at the frustrated girl, saying that she could not leave work ahead of time. Finally, the mother-in-law agreed to pick up the granddaughter Lila from the kindergarten. But instead of taking the child home to feed and comfort her, Alena's mother-in-law dragged the tired and scared girl to the prison. Alena's daughter saw the mother in the window, was eager to get to her, and began to scream. But the guards did not allow Alena meet her two-year-old child or to explain her that she is not coming home. The mother-in-law with force dragged Lila away holding her hand, not even trying to calm and comfort her. Instead, looking at Alena, mother-in-law was simply annoyed and shouting angrily: "What will I do with your child? I have to work! " Despite the recent new quarrel with her own mother, Alena knew that she really loved her granddaughter. Then in despair, she called out to her mother-in-law: "Take my daughter to my mother." This heartbreaking scene forever cut into the memory of Alena, tormenting her with a feeling of constant guilt. Lila also remembered it forever.

***

Only at the end of the day a rather young, assertive and very rude investigator Nosova came to prison. In an objectionable tone, the investigator began to ask Alena insulting questions. With condemnation, she began to claim that Alena tried to hide from justice and did not appear for interrogations on many calls. Alena, with tears in her eyes, made excuses, saying that she really did not know anything about the summons for interrogation. She tried to explain that she had long moved to live in another place, then went to the university in the other city, then spent almost a month in the hospital. But the tough investigator did not believe her. Alena really did not understanding why she was arrested. She only repeated that she was not going to hide from anyone. In the end, she was told that she was charged under Article 138 for the defamation. At that moment of cruel and baseless accusation, she felt hopeless despair. The bitter, deep loneliness again swept the soul of the tormented girl. And she just cried out childishly, not knowing that everything was just beginning.

It turned out that at the request of her high-ranking uncle, her family decided to support his lawsuit in order to punish Alena for the insulting letter. Moreover, at the request of her own relatives, it was decided to check the girl with a forensic psychiatrist for sanity. To do this, they planned to send her, like any criminal to the Krasnodar prison. She had to stay in that horrible cell, and wait when enough criminals would be gathered from all over the district to form a train.

After a hysterically-nagging meeting with her little daughter, Alena was taken to a gloomy, damp and cold cell. This dark, windowless, with blank walls cement cell was about 6 x 3 meters in size. One of the ice walls had a small bare and cement elevation for sleeping. In the corner was a stinky barrel (bucket) for the toilet. It was necessary to manage to do everything into it by somehow sitting on a high dirty edge, without falling into the barrel. In the morning, the prisoners rolled out these barrels to empty them.

50

At that time there, one of the guards was Alena's classmate - Sasha Varchenko. It turned out to be a huge shock for him to suddenly see a "star of his class" locked up as a banal crime in a dirty cold cell. For Alena, it was a shameful, but still comforting luck. She immediately asked him first to send the library textbooks that were with her during the arrest, and return them to the university. She also explained that she had recently been in the hospital, and still had a fever. She asked her classmate to bring her something warm, bypassing all their prison rules. She needed to hide from the cold and damp of that cell. To her surprise, he, a kind soul, did all this, but said that in the morning his shift would end and the other guards would take it all away.

After some time, the guards put another woman to the same cell with Alena. That woman suddenly jumped like a crazy on Alena back and grabbed her hair. Alena began to scream wildly. Security came running, and this crazy woman was taken away. And a day later, a young and very frightened girl Tanya appeared there. She was arrested almost naked right on the beach. When she abandoned her fleeting lover, he stated that she had robbed him. And in order to take revenge on her, he attracted his local friends to this, as his "witnesses."

Tatyana was all shaking from the cold and horror of her hopeless situation. She was threatened with two years in prison under Article No. 144 for the robbery. In order to at least somehow console her, Alena gave her thin blanket, which had been brought the day before by her former classmate. Suddenly, at night, strange sounds began to be heard from a neighboring chamber. Tatyana took an iron mug that was given with the tea the day before, put an ear to it, and began to listen. Then, to Alena's great surprise, in response, she too began to gently tap something with the spoon left after a meager dinner.

In a nearby cell two local young men, repeat thieves, sat, waiting for a transfer, as well. Under the ceiling of Alena's cell, there was a small hole. Soon, they began to quickly disassemble it. Late at night, the hole was large enough. Then one of the guys, smiling broadly and gleaming with a mouthful of golden teeth, climbed into the girls' cell. His partner, too, was already half in the same hole, hanging down. But then suddenly a night detour began. Guards saw him, pulled out and started to beat. His heavy moans rolled throughout the prison. And Tatyana, hiding in a corner, whispered: "Now they will come for us, and they will also beat us."

There was so much fear on her face that she almost turned gray and began to lose consciousness. Alena still twisted in her own beautiful world, considering herself not guilty of anything. She, even in prison, continued to live in the bright illusions and ignorance about real life. Despite her sad situation, Alena still strangely believed in the goodness and justice of the world. She sacredly believed in her guiding star and guardian angel. She could not imagine such atrocities as the beating of women in prison, she could not believe in such cruelty towards her, the beautiful queen of the Greek tribes of Gelendzhik. This time, the girls were lucky. The guards did not come for them. Nothing physical was done for the pacification of the two fools who were flirting with bandits even in the bullpen.

***

Only two weeks later, a special train was assembled to deliver avid criminals to be taken to a regional prison. There were so many women in the cramped car behind bars that not only was there nowhere to sit, but even movement was difficult. Women spent the entire long, eight-hour journey standing. In order to go to the toilet, which located at the end of the car, women had to beg the guard for a long time. Women with shame, a mournful voice, humiliatingly asked him about this vital necessity. The most proud of them endured for as long as they could. There were those who, in spite of everyone, just did all they needed right on the floor of the car. Upon arrival at the Krasnodar Regional Prison, all those arrested were taken to the courtyard, and their names with numbers of articles were read out. Some prisoners reacted to Alena's article 138 with the surprise and curiosity. But others hastily gasped, when someone exclaimed: "That is the political one!"

After the roll call of each arrested, they asked everyone to strip naked. The women-guards rewrote everything that every person had, put their belongings in a bag, and send it to the storage until the day of the release. Then, they began a humiliating search of the bodies. Overseers in gloves, brazenly and without shame, touched the women in all intimate places, forcing them to bend down. Instead of civilian clothes, they were all given the same prison clothes (bathrobe and shawl). The prisoners received a mattress, a metal mug and a spoon. And then, everyone was sent to a common cell, where there were already more than thirty women.

Entering a huge cell with windows under the ceiling, Alena in fear stopped at the door, listening to the energy of noise, looking around for a quiet place. But several women surrounded her and began to ask why she got into these troubles. Confused Alena did not answer all this turmoil. Her beautiful face looked lost, and her huge brown eyes glowed with grief. Moreover, she didn't know exactly what article No. 138 was about. So, she only nodded in response to the prisoners 'guesses. Two elderly women, ousting everyone else, took Alena to the center of the room, and indicated her place for the night. It was the second tier of the bunk bed, on the metal mesh of which they helped Alena to throw her heavy mattress.

Soon, well and cleanly dressed, beautiful Alena became a prison legend, with special ghosts and inviolability. It was another good luck. For some reason, two elderly prisoners clearly patronized her, protecting from all sorts of duties, usually imposed on new ones. But the very situation and the existence of Alena in a noisy cell, with screams, swearing and fights of inveterate criminals, were terrible for her. In order, that the prisoners would not "stretch" their legs ahead of time, for the whole day they got half a loaf of stale, black bread, one herring and liquid porridge. The food was so scarce that the always graceful Alena lost weight quickly and dangerously. As her grandmother would say, she became just "skin and bones".

One could only dream of silence, peace or solitude there. The most annoying thing was the inability to occupy oneself with something. Everything was forbidden: books, newspapers, any correspondence with the outside world, any communication or meetings. This was a special punishment for everyone under investigation. But even in the complete isolation of a formidable prison, the wildest prisoners still managed to keep secret correspondence with the other prisoners. They did this with the help of ropes and window leaves, even somehow communicating with those who were outside the prison, receiving information and advice on what and how to say during interrogations.

Everyone was taken out for walks twice a week. When the women were taken outside, the guards began search the cells. Each cell was carefully examined and turned upside down. Before that, the guard in a rude voice ordered the prisoners to turn to the wall and hold their hands behind their backs. Alena was not used to obeying rude shouts, and this procedure seemed terribly humiliating to her. So, along the way, walking along the corridor, she gradually dropped her hands. And for some reason, the guards did not even pull her for it, as if realizing that she was not like everyone else. The yard for walks was small, with a closed, high, dull concrete fence, and barbed wire at the top. There were special observation towers at the top of the walls, and armed guards walked around, just like in a movie. In this empty courtyard, in a circle, without stopping or talking, the arrested were supposed to walk. Walking was at least some kind of entertainment. Alena was glad to breathe fresh air, to be in silence, to see the blue sky and rare birds having fun in the wild.

***

Complain

One week later, a medical commission arrived at the prison, and Alena was summoned for examination. After asking a few simple questions, and not finding a mental disorder, they diagnosed "healthy." Then another week passed, but everything was unchanged. Alena began to think that her cruel imprison without a trial has been going on for ages. This prison was in a big, unfamiliar city, where there were neither her friends nor a lawyer. Alena did not have any meetings with her relatives, and there were no additional transfers of food so necessary in the prison. It seemed that everyone had forgotten about her, and the other life that she had before did not exist at all.

But "on the day of complaints" the guards put several pieces of paper and he pencils into the cell. But only few women prisoners interested in them, not believing in success. Alena felt deeply and unjustly punished, and she had nothing to lose. In addition, to her natural optimism, living since childhood in an eternal struggle, Alena was accustomed to use every little chance to improve her life. "What if something good comes out of my complaint and somebody helps me," she thought. She decided to describe her terrible story and the ill-treatment she faced.

By some miracle, this letter was handed over to the chief prosecutor of the Krasnodar. He was very surprised at such a strange incident with an intelligent girl. Apparently, having decided that the Gelendzhik bureaucrats had exceeded their authority, he ordered to improve Alena's conditions in his prison, and send her as soon as possible back to Gelendzhik. The authorities of the regional prison were worried by the intervention of the prosecutor. Soon Alena was transferred to a very small, but quiet, cell for six people.

***

In this new cell for the "intelligentsia," special women, whom they called "millionaires", were sitting under investigation. As it became clear from their conversations, they once worked in the privileged, "Resort Torg", corrupted, and controlled, by a local mafia. There, Alena's mother and her aunt worked, as well. But these arrested prisoners were accused of embezzlement of huge sums of money, of fraud with food and of speculation. In addition the most terrible thing for them was that they were accused of bribery, as well as in the "theft of Soviet property" on an especially large scale.

The investigation had been going on for several years. All this time they were sitting in a tight cell, without the right to see someone, receive newspaper, or any letters. They were like "privileged" prisoners, because they had great connections to the very high people outside. Even some high ranks in Moscow were connected to them and their crime. These ties went to the very top of society, and maybe government. And no one knew how all this could turn out. Therefore, with them, with the "millionaires", everything was very mysterious and difficult. They even went for a walk separately from the rest of the prisoners.

First, they met young Alena coldly, wary, but politely. In this cell, rarely did anyone swear, and there was no negative, frenzied, desperate energy, as there was in the previous big cell. So, it was already a relief for Alena's esthetics. However, at first, the women thought that Alena was planted for them on purpose, that she might be a spy. Therefore, they communicated among themselves in some incomprehensible, conditional language. But Alena did not ask them anything, and did not talk at all, busy with her thoughts. So, they soon relaxed a bit, and generally stopped paying attention to the young cellmate

Once Alena was horrified to see that they were often taken to interrogations. After that they returned, barely dragging their legs, bruised, with battered hair and abrasions. They courted each other sympathetically, slowly coming to a "normal" state, as it were before. And then, at leisure, they played their homemade cards or tell fortunes on cards guessing about the future. They taught Alena how to play the card game "Preference", the main entertainment of the prison.

In this creepy cell, with fat, weak and battered women, Alena became a witness to their difficult life stories. Sharp in her mind and observant, she realized that they were still hoping that they would be rescued by "Iron Bela". They respectfully mentioned the name of Bela, calling her Naumovna. Upon learning that Alena's mother also worked in the "Resort Torg", the prisoners stopped hiding something from the innocent looking Alena. But she did not tell them that this sonorous name of Bela had been familiar to her since childhood. Her mother was friends with the almighty Bela, who handled millions around maybe the whole Soviet Union. Bela even sometimes visited Emma's new home, always bringing something special. She beautifully smiled, amiably talking quietly with her grandmother. After Bela's visits, life in the parental home became calmer and more comfortable.

But, as it turned out later, Bela could not help her former co-workers, prisoned for the crime they committed together. Soon, she was also arrested and brutally tortured. "High posts" made Bela a "scapegoat", cleaning, sweeping their own criminal traces, hiding their own crimes. She was shot in 1982, having survived Alena's mother for only three years.

***

Punishment

Alena spent a hard month in a Soviet investigative prison. She saw there too much bad stuff and heard all that usually happens in such places. Having been released, she never told anyone about what was happening there, in a terrible place of congestion. Sometimes she met there the innocent victims of the Soviet regime and pressure machine.

Once in Gelendzik someone gave her Solzhenitsyn's book, "One Day of Ivan Denisovich", which was banned in the Soviet Union. This small work of a banned immigrant described very accurately what Alena herself personally experienced in the prison. But the guardian angel hovered over Alena, and her "miracles in the sieve" continued. Apparently thanks to the written complaint, Alena was soon returned to Gelendzhik. She gave a recognizance not to leave, and was left alone before the trial. At her mother's house she found her little daughter Lila, who also needed love and care. Lila was insanely happy to see her mother. And only in the tender affection of her daughter, Alena drew her strength to continue her life. Right after her arrest, Alena was fired from her previous job at the Research Institute of Sea Geophysics. In the small town, where everyone knew each other, it was very difficult to find any job. But Alena, overcoming depression, began to prepare for her defense in the court.

At this time, her first husband, Sergei, was still in Novosibirsk. He did not know anything about the sad situation of his former classmate and the mother of his daughter. His parents did not tell him anything, "for his own good," as his mother said. But when on the day of his birth on October 28 he did not receive the expected congratulatory telegram from Alena, Sergei called his parents and asked about her. And only then they reported what had happened to his wife. Soon, he flew to Gelendzhik and began to collect the money for Alena's very expensive lawyer.

The moral-indicative court was prepared quickly. Sudden imprisonment, heinous examination in the neuropsychiatric dispensary, all was organized by relatives as a punishment for Alena. Now, the main thing for her uncle, who started this, was that, she had to be formally convicted and be punished. With her conviction, he planned to be rehabilitated at his work. And his career, damaged by her insulting letter, could somehow recover.

All Gelendzhik relatives came to court, except for the relatives of her husband. Alena stood in the courtroom, surrounded by a condemning crowd, not seeing any protection or salvation. Only once did she turn back and look at her mother, who was sitting with her eyes downcast. Then she looked at her beloved grandmother with bitter pursed lips, and at the grinning stepfather. All of them participated in this conspiracy, in this performance. In the testimony, the stepfather tried the most. He struggled to look for unfavorable examples from her past, trying to prove that she was always a problem child. Alena, looking at her "family", could not believe that her seemingly close people demanded for her a terrible punishment. All her many years of illusions, the expectations of their understanding and love, everything was destroyed.

A terrible fire of revenge flared up in Alena's soul. She could no longer forgive her relatives for all the cruelty with which they had treated her all her twenty years. They crossed the line of no return, and Alena's heart almost did not feel any love for them. For a moment, her eyes flashed with a terrible fire of despair. Then, the incredible stream of a strange energy of destruction flew from her eyes towards her relatives. But it was too late to regret about anything.

The lawyer Bogdan faithfully worked for the entire amount paid to her. From a variety of people, she collected a lot of positive reviews about Alena. To them she attached numerous diplomas and letters of commendation, which the girl received annually from various public organizations for her activity. Friends and several scientific leaders from her previous job (where everybody loved Alena) came to this court hearing. They spoke highly of the girl's personality and her diligent work. All that she was accused of sounded ridiculous, and did not fit with the beautiful appearance of an intelligent beauty.

Then, in order to make a more negative impression on the judge, the prosecutor began to read offensive quotes from the letter that Alena had sent her uncle to work. Despite the truthfulness of the facts, the rudeness of the expressions and the emotional coloring with which the letter was read out loud, they did not fit the appearance of a fragile girl. Everything sounded very unsightly. Alena's face was burning with shame, and she quietly cried from this public humiliation. One of her former and brave colleague rose from his seat. He said loudly, that even the most insulting letter with half the truth that sounded here, was still not such a big crime for which you could just grab a man on the street and send him to prison. But he was immediately and sharply stopped. His ardent, protective speech was immediately and rudely interrupted. He got a clear threat, and humbly sat down.

***

In Soviet times, a passport and a "records of work book" were the main documents of any person. By virtue of Russian laws, if a person was under investigation, a court, or a condemning a sentence, all of it led to a shameful stamp and a record in a special "records of work book". The fatal record of one of the event in the "record of work book" was the worst punishment. It was for a lifetime. In that heyday of "communist stagnation" with such a record, a person was forever marked with a black, indelible stain. He could never get a good job. Learning about it too late, Alena's mother dragged her to the police chief to ask him not to make such a terrible record, not to break the fate of a young girl. Everyone in the city knew and respected Emma. She was always kind and responsive to all, and helped many with scarce goods. In addition, she was a friend of the famous "Iron Bela", with whom she worked together. Everyone tried to please "Iron Bela" and her friends.

At that time, universal mutual responsibility, a bribe was in the order of things, and it was used to achieve success in any business. It all depended only on the purpose and size of the bribe. This visit to the chief of police was no exception, because fate of the daughter was at stake. So mother Emma presented the chief of police with imported warm leather gloves. At that time, in a country of continuous deficit, this was a generous gift. Gloves like this were impossible to find anywhere. Then, they simply and unconcernedly talked about this and that. The police chief smiled happily from his unlimited power. Alena sat nearby, burning with shame. But the fateful record was not made.

In Alena's tormented soul, no one could erase the horror that she experienced in all these trials. An indelible mark of family betrayal and an abusive court forever remained in her soul a bleeding wound. Many painful years of suffering and bitter wanderings have passed. Forgiveness in Alena's soul was finally found, but by this time there was no one on earth to whom she could give it.

***

After the trial, Alena was must to find a job in order to fulfil the punishment was awarded to her, and pay a huge fine to the state. To Alena's surprise, her mother-in-law helped her. Without telling anyone about Alena's conviction, she got her a job at the Sanatorium-Forest School, where she herself worked for many years. Knowing nothing about Alena's past and having no criminal record in her "record of work book", she was assigned to work as a copy machine operator.

These huge machines stood in a special room without windows. The room had a heavy metal door, which Alena always locked with a key. Next to it was another office where Alena received visitors with the job orders. In fact, there was little work and the school teachers only occasionally brought her various documents for copying. To reproduce or print copies, they brought written permission from the director of the institution. However, hazardous chemicals were used to work with these copy machines. Therefore, after work, these two rooms, for which Alena was responsible, had to be well ventilated with through air.

For this position Alena received a minimum wage of that time, only seventy rubles. In addition, accounting office took a large portion of Alena's salary to give it to the State. For her life Alena got a very small amount of money, which was even lower than the official living wage. Alena had to live on it together with her daughter.

It is interesting to recall that in Soviet times, dissidents used every opportunity to print forbidden literature somewhere. Then, "self-published" anti-Soviet material was very popular, and some people did it by reprinting banned authors. Ironically, the former 'prisoner' Alena was arranged to work in this secret office of photocopiers. Soon after, a court order for a fine arrived to her new job place. That information from the accounting office spread on gossips and rumors. Despite the fact that Alena did not have a message about the prison and court in her "record of the work book', everyone soon found out about her "criminal" experience. But they had no right to dismiss her from the job under government requirements and conditions of the court.

During the day it was boring to sit in the enclosed rooms. So, Alena rented a tape recorder from the secretary of the organization, and enjoyed the scandalous political, sharp songs of the popular singer Vladimir Vysotsky. Thinking that the walls of her office were rather thick, she turned on the tape recorder quite loudly. From her secret cabinet, the anti- soviet songs sounded very defiant.

Ironically, in the same small corridor where the copy rooms were, cleaner worker lived. She often was drunk, asked Alena to loan her some money, and hated that Alena never gave her any. Once, having gone home, Alena forgot to close the window in her "secret room". Strangely during the same night somebody got into her office and stole the tape recorder. In the morning, in a fright, Alena immediately announced about it to the administration. But no one believed her because she was "previously convicted". They immediately convened a Komsomol meeting, condemned her, deciding to expel Alena from that communist's organization for young adults. At that time, it was intended to be another humiliating punishment. In addition, the administration decreed an additional deduction from her salary to cover the cost of the lost tape recorder. Someone superbly warmed up on the naivety or negligence of Alena.

***

For almost a year Alena was forced to continue to live and work in Gelendzhik. She dreamed of a time when she could leave behind all this bedlam and disappear from that hostile town forever. But this was not the whole bitter cup that she was to drink. In Gelendzik rumors spread fast, overgrown with all sorts of absurdities. People said, "if there was a court and a verdict, it means she was guilty", and many people tried to avoid Alena.

But once, one hairdresser, admiring Alena's chic hair, invited her to participate in a regional hairstyle contest. Alena was invited to such competitions before, even in Novosibirsk, where she lived for several years with her first husband. In Alena's sad life, especially after all the previous troubles, such invitation was a huge event. And she happily agreed. Leaving for the whole day of the competition in the neighboring city of Novorossiysk, Alena took with her a red, leather bag, where she put her things. When everyone changed clothes for the performance, Alena did not notice that her neighbor also had a similar red bag, almost the same as hers. But Alena was pure and naive, and did not attach any importance to this. The competition was especially fun, noisy and beautiful. Alena was very proud that her master hairdresser with her help took second place in the region. Alena joyfully demonstrated her fashionable hairstyle and the skills of her hairdresser, walking on the red carpet under the sounds of the hall buzzing with delight. At night they returned to Gelendzhik.

A week after this trip, one evening, a group of angry women suddenly came into Alena's courtyard. They unceremoniously broke into Alena's house, waking her relatives and demanding the return of someone else's red bag. They cursed and poured mud on her, accusing her of stealing. They recalled that it was she who had already been convicted before this contest. Shocked Alena, panting from the resentment, showed them her own red bag, assuring that she could not take someone else's. But the women left as angry as they came, dissatisfied, not believing in Alena's explanations. After a while, notorious bag was found. But no one apologized to Alena. She felt that no matter what, she would never be able restore her good name in this town.

After the trial, it became completely unthinkable to live in her mother's house, as well. The stepfather continued to openly mock Alena, especially when no one was home. Once she could not stand his insults anymore. When he turned to the refrigerator, she hit him with a knife. But a short and sharp blade of a knife popped into her palm, deeply cutting her fingers. Mother called 911, Alena was taken to the hospital, and a doctor sewed up her wounds. But after the plaster cast was removed, Alena discovered that the inept doctor could not connect the tendons correctly. So, Alena's two fingers could no longer fully extend. She could not anymore play the piano, in which previously she had been fond of and found solace and oblivion from troubles. Together with the breasts extended after the childbirth, twisted fingers even more strengthened her sense of inferiority and insecurity. She struggled with it for a long time, but solved these problems much later by doing plastic surgery.

Alena's hard-working mother loved her granddaughter Lila and took care of her, as best she could. After the case with the knife, the stepfather continued to drink for weeks, slept with other women, and brought Emma pain and illness. No matter what, it all came down to one conclusion: Alena had to leave home once and for all. And mother said to Alena's face, that she could not live in this house. Needing money, Alena began selling furniture and carpets from her part of the parental home. Her mother, with a face dark from grief, stood at the window. She looked at things disappearing from her house but, for some reason, did not stop her daughter, wounded from childhood. Having finally completed the Gelendzhik period, in desperation Alena flew with her daughter again to her first husband in Novosibirsk. It was her bitter, repeated mistake. There she was stuck in poverty, cold and hunger for another two years. But then, with the great effort, she was able to get to Leningrad.

While Alena's mother was alive she gathered whole family around her. Every year, all her relatives from all over Russia were attracted by Emma's smiling, generous character and hospitality and visited her house on the warm Black Sea. But she was terminally ill for more than ten years, and partial operations did not help. After her terrible death of Alena's mother, grandmother Anna tried to gather all relatives nearby, continuing to bind them into a single whole. But when she was gone, everything fell into pieces, which there was no one else to collect.

***

Seagull

An elegant and very young girl stands at the stern of a small boat and feeds the seagulls. She has a classic Greek profile, giving her face an exquisite uniqueness. A black, wet swimsuit almost completely envelops her flexible, snake-like body. That swimming suit, like the skin of a dolphin, perfectly outlines its soft, classic contours. The sun caresses her tanned skin, slightly covered with small, white spots of salt from a recent swim in the sea. A light, warm wind plays with her long, brown hair. Her beautiful curls drift lushly on the shoulders, flow in the wind like wings.

A passenger boat rushes along the Black Sea, forming behind a white foam of waves. Sea gulls circle around the ship. They pick up pieces of bread on the fly, which are thrown to them by the young beauty. And the girl thinks that she is one of these gulls, and has fun spinning with her friends. She, too, is absolutely free, and soars easily on her wide-spread wings. When she gets tired, she can simply lie down on a fresh, elastic stream of sea air and relax. And the wind will just carry her behind the ship. More than anything, she adores her bewitching freedom, this salty, caressing wind and the shining sea.

Here she looks around the vast expanse of the sea. From above everything is clearly visible to the horizon. And she can see deep down as well, almost to the bottom, where there are a lot of different tasty fish. Watching the fish below underwater is also exciting and enjoyable. The girl is embraced by inner joy from the feeling of extraordinary freedom and the expectation of something magical that is bound to happen. This boundless joy overwhelms her, makes her unusually happy. Her whole soul sings, full of hope and expectation.

The hot blood of her Greek ancestors flows in her, and her whole essence is eager to accomplish something extraordinary. She looks at the blinding sun and cries from her overwhelming feelings, from the sensation of this unforgettable moment, which will never happen again. On this beautiful, hot, summer day, she recalls her favorite book, "Jonathan

Livingston Seagull". She cries from her unbridled thirst for freedom. She cries about her beautiful, so innocent and young life, flying so quickly over the horizon

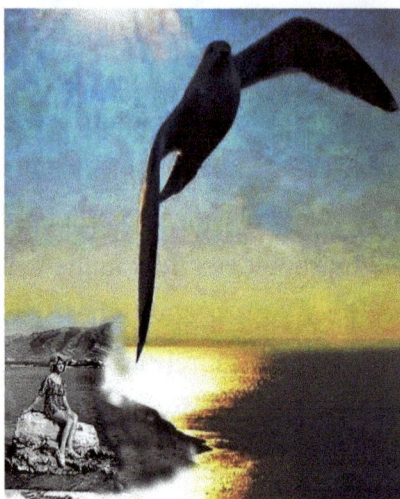

***

Part 2. Leningrad

Alena went to live in Leningrad, dreaming of a beautiful and more intellectual life in the northern capital. But to stay more than one month in this stunning city was only possible with official registration at the police office. The path to this was only through marriage, and Alena began looking for a suitable person. Soon, she met a thirty-three-year-old Jew named Sergei Berz, same as her first husband. Sergey was never married, lived comfortably with his mother, and worked as a theater director. "That chance could be successful", thought Alena, and did her best to charm him to accelerating her marriage. But his habit of freedom did not harmonize with Alena's ideas about devotion and fidelity. Moreover, as Alena quickly learned, his imperious mother, who loved to control everything around her, supported the free life of her son, indulging his whims. In everything, Alena depended on their quirks, and had to put up and adapt to their rules and way of life.

The vulnerable girl, who had already lived a hard life, needed love and tenderness and could not abide new humiliation. In addition, the independent character of Alena (Aquarius) did not endure any restrictions. The proud temper of a Greek woman, who grew up in complete freedom, did not allow her to be comfortable with the role of a maid or just a housekeeper. One year in the tiny apartment was full of differences, struggles, and effort to get rid of Alena and her little daughter. Then, her second husband and his mother realized that they couldn't just simply push and throw Alena back to Gelendzhik. Unable to get rid of her, the second Sergey filed for divorce. However, according to the law and the court order, they were forced to provide Alena with her small daughter a good size room. So, finally, Alena got her own living space in the city of her dreams.

***

Artist

Shortly after the second divorce, once at the Hermitage, Alena met a surprisingly attractive guy with huge, burning eyes and long hair, hair to the shoulders. This handsome man turned out to be a very talented artist named

Valery. He had just arrived in Leningrad from Ukraine, and enrolled in a restoration school. Apparently, he also dreamed of registering in this city.

This time Alena was lucky to meet a very good, kind and pleasant man. They both were only twenty-five years old, and Alena was his first woman. Most importantly, he was an interesting conversationalist and Alena enjoyed listening and talking to him. At that time, as always, Alena worked a lot and needed some help. Valery happily spent time with her eight-year-old daughter, took Lila from school and helped her to do homework. Soon Valery became a simply irreplaceable friend, and they got married.

Alena and Valery lived happy together for ten years. But, despite his calmness and kindness, Alena often could not rely on him. Valera was in the habit of promising something, but not fulfilling his promises. Looking into his beautiful black eyes, Alena tried to trust him, but all his promises turned out to be lies. He always had in mind to do good things, but he just could not accomplish what he promised. In addition, he did not want to officially work anywhere, explaining that his desire was to paint pictures and be just an artist.

Finally, Alena arranged for him to work at the school, where her daughter was studying. But soon after, he began to date an English teacher there. For little Lila, the betrayal of the man whom she considered her "father" was a great grief. Alena also could never forgive anyone for the broken promises to be faithful. One day, her eyes were opened to her husband's infidelity. Then, she managed to immediately unregister him out of her wonderful apartment and changed the locks. Valery was too slow, and first did not want to fight nor try to exchange an apartment. He did not have the courage or strength to use the law in order to get a room or his share through the court. Knowing Alena's strong character he did not want to fight at all with her. He simply moved to his friend, taking with them their dog Brake and their cat Tosha. When he began to fight for his room, it was too late. Alena had already sold that apartment.

During "perestroika", unable to do anything but painting, Valery could not find employment in Leningrad (St. Petersburg). He did not know where to apply himself or how to make money. Several times he borrowed money from Alena, but did not repay it. And then she, out of old friendship, and feeling sorry for Valery, tried to help him, giving him work as her driver. But, not accustomed to work somewhere regularly, Valery did not like it, and soon quit this job.

In the end, Valery was completely disappointed in the circumstances of his collapsed life in St. Petersburg. He abandoned his dog Brake to his friend, and the dog soon died, unable to bear separation from his former beloved family. And Valery, grabbing his cherished cat, went to his homeland to live in his mother's house. Finally, there he was able to find his way, painting the walls and creating the icons of the local cathedral. Alena later, already living in America, the country of her dreams, wrote a book about her youth, Russian life, and about Valery's early, Leningrad work.

***

***

Crossroads

Russian communist propaganda has generated many negative stereotypes about capitalist countries. In the 1960s and 1970s, English and military training were compulsory subjects in schools. On the radio and in newspapers they constantly talked about the threat of war with the United States. For almost seventy years, Russian citizens lived under the invisible "Iron Curtain," with virtually no opportunity to travel abroad. Only Russian Jews could obtain permission to immigrate to Israel. Many beautiful stereotypes were created about the unattainable and wonderful life abroad. Some who went abroad on business trips, seafarers, and their wives created these tales. Greatly exaggerated, almost fantastic tales of a beautiful and prosperous life abroad grew everywhere. And then, they were also enhanced by Hollywood films. Especially the country of paradise - USA, inaccessible to most Russian people, was praised the most. Like many others, Alena grew up in Russia with the thought that America is the only place where everyone wants to immigrate.

During the communist time, getting to know foreigners was undesirable and suspect. This was regarded as treason and betrayal of the homeland. Women who met with foreigners were monitored and severely punished. They were most often forced to "work" for the State Security Committee, and report to the KGB details of their exchanges and conversations with foreigners. Alena was not from a Jewish family who would be allowed to emigrate. For all non-Jews, there was only one legal way to leave the country: to marry a foreigner. However, Alena was fed up with her previous forced marriages, and had no good reason to do it. The very thought of marriage was disgusting to her.

In the early 1990s, Russia began an extraordinary, dramatic transformation initiated by President Mikhail Gorbachev. After the failed coup of the Communists, supporters of Yeltsin's hard line, a disastrous decision was made to dissolve the Soviet Union. Many described the situation in Russia at that time as a "tragedy of historical proportions." In fact, in the 1990s the economic situation in Russia worsened. People who worked hard still did not receive a salary of more than forty dollars a month.

At this time, Alena lost her favorite work as a museum guide. Nevertheless, she was more fortunate than most people because she had many true friends and excellent connections. But most importantly, she was very hardworking and optimistic. One day, one of her enterprising friends invited her to join their new pharmaceutical business. There has always been a shortage of medical drugs in Russia, and such a business promised to be very profitable. Therefore, Alena did not think too long and grabbed luck by the tail. She boldly invested most of her savings in this new business, and devoted all her time to the new work.

Life tempered the character of Alena. But her appearance still retained the features of a holy, pure Madonna. In 1995, she was almost forty, but she underwent plastic surgery and looked very young. In addition, her many friends and fans considered her a smart, well-read, highly educated and successful business woman. That's improved her self-esteem. Despite the fact that she already seemed to have lived a long life, her soul was still young, full of hope and kept the thirst for life.

During the "perestroika" Alena felt that she had finally achieved everything that seemed to be possible for an enterprising woman in Russia. By this time, she had a high income, she was provided with everything, and did not depend on anyone. She became an independent business lady. Thanks to her energy and desire to overcome all obstacles, her business quickly began to gain momentum. Soon a dizzying success came to her, and Alena firmly stood on her feet. By the mid-1990s, she was already able to buy two cars, as well as a second apartment for her daughter in the same building where she lived. Moreover, when most people only dreamed of having a vacation on the sea at least once in their life, Alena several times a year took her family to Italy, Malta and Greece.

Soon in Greece her daughter met a young guy, who not only was dating Lila, but also was interested in selling his fur coats in the big cities of Russia. Lila began to do it with him. The money she earned gave her an excellent life for some time. It is also took a burden off Alena's shoulders, for she had supported her daughter and granddaughter all her life. However, soon uncontrolled gangsters put the entire small business in Russia at risk. In St. Petersburg, it was dangerous to store valuables in your home. Once, Lila's apartment with several fur coats was looted.

In order to survive this dangerous time, Alena tried to work as quietly as possible, trying to hide her profitable business from racketeers and gangsters. She brought her scarce medical goods for sale only to some of the surviving factories, which people could access only by special pass. There, under the protection of police guarding the entrance, she worked in the lobby having her temporary mobile kiosk. But this did not last long. The field of activity narrowed, fear grew, and business suffered losses. Several times Alena's elderly, loyal driver and the bodyguard were caught and beaten and the money was stolen. After that, they left the job, leaving Alena alone. It was difficult for her to find a new driver or new places where would it be easy and safe to sell the medicine. Her savings were getting low.

With each new day, it became increasingly difficult for her to live alone, supporting a comfortable lifestyle, which she greatly valued. But if she stopped earning every day, then all her savings would disappear very quickly. And in St. Petersburg there was still the same cold climate, slush, endless rains, gloomy skies, dirty streets and empty shops. No money could compensate for the unpleasant social conditions and unsightly habitat.

Of course, Alena could still go to live in her Gelendzhik, where she grew up. The resort town was especially pleasant from April to October. The warm gentle sea and the sun always quickly restored Alena's strength, removing any spiritual burden. But in a small town there was practically no work. In the most beautiful city of her childhood, with amazing nature and climate, there were too many bitter memories. Only the graves of her relatives awaited her there. Alena could not even walk the streets without pain and tears.

Then Alena thought even more deeply about where to arrange her life more comfortably and more stably.

***

Having lived a life very full of emotions, events and work, Alena was sure that she deserved more than she had in Russia. She traveled a lot and was a "citizen of the world". As a result, she thought she had experienced and known life in foreign countries. She was confident in herself, believing that she could easily live in any place, and that she would not have difficulties with adaptation anywhere. She did not realize at that time that being a tourist and living constantly in an unfamiliar country are two different things.

At the same time, unscrupulous deceivers who succeeded in all kinds of frauds thrived in Russia. It became especially popular to open marriage dating agencies. There, trusting Russian women, for high fees, were offered "quickly and safely" to marry a foreigner for improving their lives.

Leningrad (Saint Petersburg) has always been a city of tourists. After the "perestroika", there were especially many foreign tourists, and the opportunity to communicate with them became much more accessible. In addition, Alena was a guide, and constantly working with people; she had the skills of easy communication with any person. Being a curious and venturesome person, she decided to study foreign candidates for husbands. In this period of her prosperous life, Alena did not have to marry under duress, as before. She did not need to marry in order to better arrange her life, give birth to a child or obtain a residence permit in a big city. A new, completely exciting time has come for her. She no longer needed a man to help her, or to use him as an elevator to move on to a higher quality of life. And this was a relief. It seemed that she could freely choose the one she wanted, according to her taste and desire.

However, over time and with the growth of her well-being, the requirements for the spiritual and emotional qualities of men increased. Her plans did not include adjusting to the lower spiritual level of a man. Her man needed to be a smart and attractive person, not a cheater or a shriveled freak. Moreover, Alena had no desire to move to the apartment of a man who lived with his mother, or to share with him her own apartment. She could not imagine life with an old or constantly grumbling man, especially if he made less money than she.

Now, Alena, with her deep emotionality, originality, expressive soul, and with her exceptional requirements for a man, it has become even more difficult to get along with anyone else. It has become even more difficult for her to find a good guy with whom it would be interesting spend time together, who would satisfy her spiritual and emotional essence, without constantly demanding sex. Alena understood that only compromises make a marriage truly happy. But she could not decide which of the above she could sacrifice for a new marriage.

As often happens, successful and attractive women of forty years old liked younger men. But Alena often met gigolos or controlling despots. At parties where Alena was often invited, around the graceful, elegant and smart woman the successful "new" Russians circled. They got rich in the wake of "perestroika," and not always in a legitimate or pure way. These young guys were often spoiled upstarts, without education, good manners, or simply arrogant bandits, without morality and principles. Money for them had the main value, and was the meaning of life. They were not shy in the means for their achievement. These categories of men could not be a good choice for partnership or Alena's next marriage.

Alena often met men with wrinkled faces and fatty deposits, who were too much battered by promiscuous partying, excesses, wine and cigarettes. Despite their own problems, they were still looking for a young woman or a woman without children, who would focus all her attention on them. In addition, the elderly Russian men had bad smell. Moreover, they had a very unpleasant habit of pouring their feelings and problems on a woman, using her as a psychotherapist. Alena had enough of her own internal problems and experiences, and was not interested in listening to their constant whining, or their constant digging in their own feelings. It was boring and burdensome. Despite all of the above, Alena was still a romantic person, and dreamed of meeting real, great love. The appearance of new children was excluded for her. She needed a caring person who would be absolutely faithful to her. Alena simply wanted to live easily and joyfully, without domestic or emotional problems, without fear of being deceived or betrayed. At the same time, she did not want to emigrate and depend on anyone in a foreign country.

After carefully considering all the options, she sent her ad to a special magazine where men wanted to find a Russian wife. Thousands of letters came to Alena from different countries. Among them were many tempting offers. Now she just had to choose a prosperous country where she could live without problems and worries.

***

Paris

In general, Russians are very kind, gullible, hospitable and open people. But before the "perestroika" they practically did not go abroad, and least of all knew something about America, except for some stereotypes from the movies. In Russian magazines, American men were portrayed with large cigars. It was said that they do not like to work, but only play golf. Travel circles confirmed that most American tourists were fat, slow, uneducated, and arrogant.

After the "perestroika", many foreign adventurers and elderly lovers of young girls flooded Russia in search of easily accessible, naive women. Alena's friends often warned her that only losers with some sexual, financial, economic or personal problems try to find a lowly bride in third world countries. Such men were confident that a woman from a poor country would be more flexible, accommodating and cheap. They suggested that she would easily put up with all the problems encountered in their countries, would not be demanding or controlling, as their local women were.

Such talk about foreigners looking for cheap brides bothered Alena. When she received letters from candidates for a Russian wife, she tried to find the catch in their letter. Any letter immediately showed the character of their author, and some of the messages seemed pretty smart. Others tried to be even more thoughtful. They put in the envelop one dollar for the postage for the "bride" to reply. It was good, and such letters got initial attention.

But first of all, Alena looked through letters with photos, choosing men according to their facial expressions. The face of each person reflects his character and his lifestyle.

There were so many letters that to view all of them took several hours a day. Most letters were written by hand in foreign language. Poor knowledge of English and slow translation with a dictionary took too much time. Some letters had many tempting offers, but it was a laborious process, which took a lot of effort and valuable time. The previous marriages and life experiences taught Alena to not trust the intentions of all these men.

It became apparent that relationships at a distance or through letters are a hopeless illusion that could bring unpleasant surprises. Then, it turned out that the local "Dating Bureau" had long become just pimps earning from the use of gullible women for their own quick enrichment.

In addition, soon the postal office people also realized that there was money in the envelopes. They began to open envelopes, extracting money before delivering letters. Alena did not have time or desire to study long letters from abroad, and became completely uninterested in receiving them.

Gradually, Alena realized that the fears of her friends were correct. And after several real meetings with foreigners, she finally lost all interest in such a process. On her way to a new marriage, there were too many circumstances and conditions that had to be met before she agreed to marry a new man, especially an unknown foreigner.

***

It seemed easiest to go to the capital of France. For everyone who wanted to get out of Russia during all kinds of upheavals, it was France that was the most obvious choice for emigration. Moreover, for several centuries, knowledge of French culture and language was mandatory for the Russian aristocracy and high society.

Paris was very close, in Europe, just two hours from Alena's beloved St. Petersburg. Both cities surprised with their similar architectural ensembles, built by the same architects, in the same style. Paris, like St. Petersburg, was the center of many exciting events, exhibitions and museums, magnificent parks and cultural institutions. Alena's perception of Paris was formed with the help of romantic French literature. She had read a lot, and loved Balzac, Maupassant, Dumas and other French writers. So, after the "perestroika" the first city to travel to was Paris. There she found several families of the old Russian intelligentsia - well-settled and wealthy people. And even she herself began to take private French lessons. There, in her previous trips, Alena had already met several of the applicants for her "hand and heart". It seemed to Alena that France would be her main choice for a future life, and it would be logical to settle there.

Most often, Paris met Alena with a drizzling rain, gray sky and low clouds. The climate there was also almost the same as in St. Petersburg. Alena did not feel "abroad." But when friends began to take her to chic restaurants with extremely high prices, she soon felt that she could not afford it. This lifestyle was not for her. Also, on the streets of Paris, she was not free at all, or incognito, as in St. Petersburg. She could not walk alone or disappear into the crowd, enjoying something, without the intrusive attention of men. One winter, putting on her magnificent mink coat, Alena went for a walk along the Champs Elysees. It stretches from Concorde Square to the Arc de Triumph, about 1915 meters easily walkable. This is a very pleasant place for a walk, with the shining lights of decorated trees, attractive shop windows and cafes. But when Alena got to Concord Square, a car stopped right next to her. An elegantly dressed man, smiling amiably, offered to give her a lift to the hotel. But soon after Alena got in, he turned to the nearest underground parking and began to annoyingly offer to have sex for an impressive fee. It sounded as it was normal for him, as if it was in the order of things. But such a discovery shocked Alena, and she stopped going for walks alone the beautiful streets of Paris.

Soon Alena realized that everything was for sale in the capital of Europe. Fleeting sex was the main motive and stimulus for the life of devastated people. Paris, as it was sung in the famous song, "day and night, burned in a circular passion, when the fatal force conquered new lips, carrying away the illusion of a beautiful dream." It was a constant carnival in the late hours of the Paris nights. It seemed that men did not have any significant hobbies, nor exciting work. It seemed that they did not think about anything substantial, did not value anything but good food and sex. Obviously, most of them were bored, had nothing to occupy themselves with, and they were looking for daily adventures. Soon Alena was very tired of the carefree Parisians. She met apparently very superficial, living just one day wealthy and spoiled, but such weak men of Paris.

In her repeated visits to Paris, she was still trying to assess how good French men could be for a stable, lasting relationship and marriage. But time passed without a tangible positive result. And the French were elegant dandies, who loved themselves most of all, and who did not plan "serious intentions". In addition, the men there competed with each other for a good woman. They drove Alena to the most expensive nightclubs, trying to make the best, as they thought, impression. One day she asked to be taken to theater or opera, to a concert, or to an exhibition. She wanted to go to more interesting and more spiritual places. But in response, she saw only their bewilderment and was very disappointed. It became clear that in Paris it was most likely good to just relax, and a good vacation required a lot of money. But a permanent life in such a carefree atmosphere was not for Alena, and soon she became very bored.

***

Visa

In Alena's favorite ancient Greek mythology, King Aegeus possessed huge herds. All of them were kept in special stables. For many years, manure was not exported from these stables, so terrible chaos was happening there. In order to clean them, King Aegeus hired Hercules. Hercules in a cunning way diverted water from two rivers there, and these rivers simply washed out all the manure.

After disappointment in the frivolous men of Paris, Alena came to the conclusion that it was time to clean the "Augean Stables". It was time to put things in order at home, in her plans, and in the head. In the mid-1990s, Alena saw that the time had come when it became much easier to overcome the obstacles to obtaining a tourist visa in the United States. Her friends helped her find one person in the government who promised to make such a visa without problems, but for good money. At that time, the real price of a tourist visa in the United States was about fifty dollars. The average salary of an ordinary Russian person was also about fifty dollars a month. And the recommended official asked to pay him a huge sum of $2,000 for a tourist visa with multiple entries into the United States.

Having decided on this, Alena began to raise money by selling all her valuables. She sold the car and gave him the money. But then another huge problem arose. A similar visa to the USA was issued only if the person had a special return ticket for the plane, although without a return date. It was a very expensive nonrefundable ticket. Alena had no other choice, but to buy such a ticket, having spent another thousand dollars to purchase it. After that, another problem arose. In fact, Alena did not know anyone in the United States. She had no idea where to go there directly from the airport, or what could be done there at all. After selling a car, an apartment and other valuables, after acquiring an expensive visa and an expensive ticket, she was in a hopeless situation. There was no turning back. Then the average "Regular Pig Bean" turned up to her. We will call him just "Regular Bean" further on.

BOOK 2. Regular Bean

From childhood Alena grew up surrounded by all sorts of secrets, and suffered from the fact that everyone was hiding something from her. This raised her suspicion and distrust of people. When she met the smallest secret, it caught the fire inside her. She could not stop until she reached the source of the mystery. This peculiarity remained in her forever.

As a child, watching others, Alena learned to notice various "coincidences", strange signs of fate, and listened to her grandmother's interpretations. From ancient times, people believed that every name of a person has a semantic load, and carries a part of the fate. Many years later, when Alena once met an American named Bob, she thought about the coincidence of his name with Russian grain. Then, she heard his last name which was very consonant with the Russian word "pig." This was a double warning sign. But she did not stop in pursuit of her goal, although later life proved to her the correctness of ancient predictions.

In the 1990s, as always before, everything was in short supply in Russia. People found uses for everything they could find in stores and rejoiced in any little things. For example, they did not have colorful plastic bags. Sometimes foreigners gave such bags to them, as a cheap souvenir. And when men presented a more "substantial" gift, like a four-color pen, or a booklet with some photos of their country, this had an even greater impression on inexperienced Russian women. So, almost any foreigner with souvenirs could easily looked like a prince, and quickly win a naive woman in a poor country. In addition, Russian women, by the simplicity of their souls, invested too much emotions and feelings in relationships with men.

As it turned out right away, "Regular Bean" had a special interest in dating Russian wealthy women. But Alena found out the truth much later. Also, "Regular Bean" enjoyed the very process of seducing women in Russia. It was easy. Local women were not spoiled by the attention of their local men. They melted from the attention of the foreigners who gave them simple souvenirs. "Regular Bean" liked the feminine admiration of his "gifts," and this raised his own pride. Thus, the jerk and rascal «Regular Bean», with many internal problems, felt like a real king in Russia. "Regular Bean" was not able to maintain a strong, long relationship with women. He did not have any opportunities or a chance. And most women apparently did not seek to share with him the little that they had in Russia, or that they brought with them to America. As a result, he quickly divorced them. So, having completed one lap, "Regular Bean" again came to Russia with the new hope. This time, he met with Alena.

Coincidentally, at the same time, the circumstances of life in St. Petersburg, the declining amount of money, and fleeting time forced Alena to act quickly. At the beginning of their acquaintance, his passion for foreigners gave Alena a chance for a successful and quick departure from Russia.

And most importantly for Regular Bean was that he did not need to spend any money for the flight ticket of this "new bride". And even more important, he did not have to apply for a Fiancé's visa, which imposed a serious ten-year responsibility on a groom for her life in America. Only several months later, already in the USA, Alena found out about the deep contrast between the behavior, status and character of Regular Bean in St. Petersburg and his daily life in his American village.

***

Shock

Any movement or travel Alena perceived as an adventure. New places meant new life. A serious move was stressful, but also a very exciting event. In December 1995, in her magnificent mink coat, Alena last walked through the sparkling New Year's lights in Paris. Then, enthusiastically she flew to California. Her soul expected all the most fabulous and beautiful in a new country. Her main dream was to create a strong and happy home and family. She did not expect new disappointments or unforeseen situations.

Alena did not know that California in the past was a desert. She recently had asthma and California was too dry for her. Also, nobody warned her that in California it is warm even in the winter, and rain and snow are very rare here. Leaving the plane in a mink fur coat and boots, Alena gasped from the heat. Then, from the car window, she saw only gray-brown fields and bare hills without any vegetation. Such a dull landscape, with its emptiness and grayness, was especially depressing. But in Russian life, she developed the habit of looking for positive aspects in everything. "It is still better than the climate with the snow", she thought.

***

Every immigrant has a difficult feeling when passing through the cultural shock of a foreign country. Alena was sure that she was a person of the World, and would adjust to the new country very fast. But in America she immediately faced the sharp emotional problem of adaptation and compromise, for which she was not ready. Her pride and her strong personality did not want to compromise. The difficult stages of adaptation took a very long time for her.

In the first weeks of her appearance in America, the biggest problem was her poor knowledge of English. In Russia, her sincere and warm communication with people has always been of great importance. It was a pleasure. "Man does not live by bread alone." All her past jobs were based on communication. Getting into a prestigious job, for example as a tour guide, was extremely difficult. In addition to her general university education, it was necessary to complete several special courses and pass a large competition. Many people dreamed about this intellectual and interesting work, but very few could get it.

During several years of her job as a tour guide, Alena had more than twenty different art topics in the museums of St. Petersburg. She worked in palaces, parks, museums, cathedrals, and took tour trips to Baltic Republics. Her deep knowledge of history, art and architecture gave her admiration and respect from her listeners, tourists from all over Russia. Every day they delighted in Alena's enthusiasm and "bathed her in complements."

In Russia, Alena's job was the whole meaning of her life, bringing satisfaction and joy. After the "perestroika", she had a different, but also very profitable, pharmacy business. The new business also had a lot of positive communication with people. Most importantly, she felt that people needed her. It was the best fulfilling feeling that anybody needed to feel happy.

However, in a foreign country, without good knowledge of the language, Alena felt as if she was from another planet or from a dark forest. Even in the most primitive society or in stores, with huge rows of various goods, she was very embarrassed. But she had a deep curiosity, and, watching everything around, tried to learn quickly. Alena, like any immigrant, compared the lifestyle and attitude of people with her native country or with what she had before. Everything in the new country was very different, and it gave it great discomfort. It was primarily because she did not have any emotional or financial support from the "Regular Bean" or her "groom", the person in whose house she settled. She had a multi-layered soul of Russian nesting dolls, which absorbed thousands of years of knowledge of the different centuries, cultures and nations. Amazing and tragic events of a thousand-year-old Russian culture, saturated with Orthodoxy, folklore, outstanding literature, music and dance, lived in the soul of Alena. But she suddenly found herself in the California desert, both literally and figuratively.

In any situation and in everything, Alena's eyes always looked for aesthetic beauty. In the first weeks of a strange American life, Alena made many new discoveries. Just recently, she enjoyed the beauty of the architectural ensembles of Paris, the royal palaces of St. Petersburg. After a magnificent Europe, where Alena spent a lot of time, she found herself in a tiny, deserted town. Comfortable and clean American villages, with 2-3-story private houses, beautiful front gardens and ever-blooming vegetation, were incredibly monotonous and boring for her. She could not see anything remarkable in the new surroundings. The provincial part of California did not meet Alena with amazing skyscrapers or chic shops. All of it could be found only in the center of some big cities. Her expectations were artificially created, and had nothing to do with reality. Many aspects of American life were distinguished by customs, philosophy, principles and values. And all this seemed to be superficial, meaningless and different than in the holy Russia.

Feeling a sharp contrast with her past life, Alena tried to console herself with the fact that she was still quite young, and could again change her life at any time. Nobody could destroy her unique inner world. The most important things were inside her heart. But she sorely missed her previous work, friends and family. In order to somehow alleviate the discomfort, she said to herself, "live and learn," and decided to do her best and study that famous America.

At the very first moment of her arriving in America, the first thing that surprised and immediately struck Alena at night was the appearance of very comfortable, clean, brightly sparkling gas stations. They even had special devices with soapy water and brushes for free, and you could wash the windows in the car. There was also a small shop where you could buy everything you needed on the road. The most convenient, there was a clean, warm toilet, as well. Moreover, she also liked American roads with many interchanges and telephone booths on the sidelines. Along the wide, level roads without pits and potholes, there were beautiful trees, shrubs and flowers planted. It was very nice to drive and enjoy the scenery.

When Alena left Russia, there were still no huge highways with clear road signs. In addition, many drivers often violated traffic regulations, creating many crashes. After the "perestroika", Alena had a successful business and hired an experienced driver who took her everywhere for pennies. But in the new country, without her own car and an American driver's license, the convenience of the beautiful roads was not a great comfort to her.

All her life in Russia, Alena remembered the empty shelves in stores, and a constant shortage of elementary things, all that was necessary for life. After the "perestroika" the life of big cities became more like life in Europe. But when she arrived in the United States, Alena was overwhelmed by the loaded shops and supermarkets. All year round, from all over the world, goods which you could only dream of were brought here. All year round it was easy to buy anything that was to your liking. None of the products anywhere disappeared. Fresh vegetables, fruits and berries, which were always so lacking in St. Petersburg, were in abundance. In addition, all products were cleanly washed and packaged in packs. Take everything ready, go home and enjoy. The service in the shops was very friendly. Most sellers always smiled, welcoming the buyer with a short conversation, so popular in the United States. It was very nice, because in Russia people constantly suffered from rude service or, more precisely, from the lack of service.

There were not many really fat people in Russia, because they worked hard, eat little, and moved a lot. Alena also arrived in a new country as thin and elegant as most Russian women. In America, she saw so many fat people as she had not seen even in Europe. Once in a restaurant five fat friends were sitting at the same table. Women were dressed in huge, shapeless pants and T-shirts. They were similar to each other, both in the manner of behavior and in the huge portions of food ordered. Only much later Alena realized that the main joy for the American provinces, the "big deal" and comfort was just this abundance and availability of delicious food.

However, for Alena American food seemed too sweet, and the portions in the restaurants were huge. Local people absorbed a huge amount of food, and perceived this "Cornucopia" as the norm. In Russia, people have learned to appreciate every piece of bread, because food has always been a big problem. Apparently therefore, Soviet propaganda inspired that food is not the most important thing in life. They told people, that one must live in the name of the lofty goals of communism and a happy future for grandchildren. Alena did not wait for this in Russia. But abroad she still missed the taste of Russian food, plain dishes and brown bread.

Moreover, in Russia, due to dirt and rain, people were forced to change clothes and shoes several times a day (when they could). They tried to dress especially elegantly for different events, like going to a theater or to a museum. In Soviet times, overweight women after forty tried not to wear trousers, especially when going outside. It was considered too masculine and indecent. In the majority of the American population Alena noticed a neglect of clothing, and this was especially annoying to her.

***

Men-Women

The most special celebration for a Russian person is the New Year. In that notorious 1995 Alena met it not only without gifts, congratulations and good wishes, but also without friends and family. Around her in California there was neither familiar, native comfort, nor a beloved, beautifully decorated Christmas tree. In the first weeks of her appearance in America, Alena yearned greatly for her homeland, for the active lifestyle that she loved so much, for her wonderful work and her exciting holidays in Europe. Most importantly, she did not have a close person with whom one could just talk. There was no person in the house, where she lived, who gave her attention or warmth. Her devoted friends and relatives remained in the distant past. Alena bitterly felt that she had burned all the bridges back. She saw that she had made an irreparable mistake by selling her car and apartment in St. Petersburg.

Her American "fiancé" had no friends and no social life. He did not go anywhere, preferring to be busy at work, and he often returned home after midnight. Unexpectedly, after an active life in St. Petersburg and fascinating travels, Alena found herself in a very sleepy, provincial town. And her fiancé lived in a parallel world of his own, completely alien to her. An insurmountable wall of intelligence, education, outlook on life, hopes and expectations was between them. He did not understand this, or tried not to notice. In any case, he did not make any efforts either to bring them together or to adapt Alena in his country. Fortunately, his brother Dan lived nearby, and was the exact opposite of Regular Bean. Dan worked as the director of a local bank. His good-natured wife Jenny was incredibly friendly and welcoming to Alena. Dan, too, seemed to be much more soulful and kinder than his relative. Maybe because he always had money in his pocket, and at home his good fat wife was always caring for him. These ordinary people immediately loved smiling and friendly Alena, and joyfully welcomed her appearance in their company. Meeting Alena at the airport in her exotic, chic, very expensive natural mink coat and boots, they laughed a little at the fact that no one had educated her to the climatic features of California. They turned out to be much more sensitive than Regular Bean. Realizing that Alena was in a foreign country without any help or a single soul mate, they gave her simple gifts, and all kinds of signs of attention. After a week, they already began to introduce her to their friends and neighbors.

***

Arriving in America, Alena ended up at the middle class of people with low income, not highly educated or well-read. For all of them, it was a big surprise for them that Alena repeatedly visited many countries of Europe. But still, most of the American men were friendly and easy to communicate with. At the same time, this could not be said of American women. It gradually became clear that most of the smart women were the "bosses". They controlled the weak men, "holding them under the heel".

Nonetheless, the main advantage of American women was their ability to maintain good relations with everyone around. Yet, despite their attractive smiles, they didn't let anyone come close to their hearts, and they never revealed their soul to anyone (which was typical for Russian women). Apparently because the women were strong and manipulative, the men around them felt helpless and lonely. They spent most of time at work and then in front of TV. Often, instead of somehow participating in the affairs of the family or taking care of the house, they devoted long hours to their computers. Secretly, they were engaged in corrupt and devastating pornography. This hobby led to the fact that they could not perceive a real woman with all her flaws, and cheated on her with virtual prostitutes. They had no strength and desire to pay attention or care to a real woman, because it was burdensome.

One elderly American, Stephen, told Alena about his long search for a foreign bride. After that, she realized how some women prey on the dreams of elderly men to find a young lover. Stephen was a naive romantic. He became a member of many dating clubs, and was invited to chat with many attractive women. Once on the Internet, he met a beautiful woman Catherine from Ukraine. She sent him her half-naked or intimate photographs and sensational video, convincing him in her love. In her active correspondence, she subtly pushed his conscience to the understanding that he should help her, describing the difficult situation in the country.

Stephen, working as the director of the plant and being a wealthy man, hoped that she would become his wife. Several times a month he sent her gifts, flowers, food and money to support her and her child. This went on for quite some time. Finally, he decided that it is the time to apply for a fiancé visa to enter the United States. But Catherine said that at the moment she cannot leave her sick mother alone, and that more money is needed for her treatment. Then the money was needed for her fur coats, for a dentist, for a kindergarten for his son, more and more. Stephen really liked her, they had phone sex, and he helped her by sending everything she asked.

In the end, she said she was likely to be able to come to Mexico for a week, and the naive Stephen bought her a plane ticket. Having a wonderful rest at one of the best resorts, having received a diamond engagement ring, a bunch of expensive jewelry and clothes, Catherine disappeared forever.

***

Alena knew how to make friends and keep friendship. She met elderly girlfriends who were interested in talking with the intellectual foreigner. It was important for them that it was nothing to envy or to worry about. Alena did not compete with them, did not have a car, money or a house. Alena's new friends took turns taking her everywhere with them, glad that she was surprised and admired everything around. Despite their selfishness towards men, many women enjoyed friendship with Alena. They often took her to their main entertainment (bowling), and taught how to roll a heavy ball along a special track in order to knock down pins in the distance. Alena even participated in a group competition. Also, struck by the aristocratic manners and exceptional politeness of the girl, Regular Bean relatives, Jenny and Dan began to invite Alena to their exclusive Club (Elks Club). There Alena met quite pleasant and more educated people with whom it was interesting to talk. They perceived Alena more as a beautiful and exotic person.

Once, the chairman of this club asked Alena to make a presentation on Russian traditions. This unexpected and pleasant request was a huge event for her. During the report, Alena tried very hard to pronounce the English words correctly, and showed them her wonderful albums about her favorite city. In this club Alena met new traditions, completely new to her. She was surprised to see that at the beginning of any business meeting, people stood up, turned to the flag, laid their hands on their hearts, and uttered aloud the "Pledge of allegiance" to their country. Each time, this patriotic act seemed unexpected and slightly confused Alena.

There was another custom that also seemed unnatural and pretentious to her. Before dinner, people held hands at the table, someone said thanks to God, and they kind of prayed together. Alena then thought that the prayer was something very personal, and this should not be demonstrated aloud. Although she was not yet an American citizen, she had to show respect for those who were nearby and their traditions. Some people especially well and sincerely pronounced such words of gratitude for the "food sent" and other blessings. Then Alena's goosebumps ran from the solemn significance of the moment. For a short period of life, left alone in the cold, soulless house of "Regular Bean" she managed to do and understand a lot.

***

Each person brings the habits of his past to a new relationship. Step by step, the quirks of one person can destroy any good relationship, if every day partners do not make efforts to communicate, preserving tenderness, kindness and understanding of the other person. At the beginning of her acquaintance with this Regular Bean, Alena turned a blind eye to his oddities and unpleasant habits. It was incredibly difficult for her, because everything that he did was the exact opposite with Alena's upbringing and culture.

The most important thing, according to Russian concepts, Regular Bean did not have a soul, or he hid it so carefully that there was nothing to talk about with him. Emotional and spiritual communication is the main connecting link for people. Moreover, Alena, with her uniqueness, had nothing in common ground with a limited Regular Bean. They did not have a common cultural layer, where they grew up, had no unifying memory.

In addition, he very often had no work at all. At such days, he got up very early in the morning, turned on the TV at full volume, and sat in front of it all day. He was frowning, in a bad mood from idleness, lack of money, and not caring at all for the sleeping woman.

From the very first day of her new life, Alena was locked in a rented house. The loneliness and silence of the house was terrible. She felt like she was in a prison. The main problem was the large distance between the villages, shops and everything around. The absence of the car reinforced its isolation, and created a feeling of emptiness. Regular Bean forbade her to talk even on a local telephone, so that she would not waste money.

Every day, Alena was left alone for the whole day with a Siamese "pest" cat named "Navel". Regular Bean got the cat from his seventh Russian wife when she divorced him. Although Alena also had a cat in St. Petersburg, her Tosha was an affectionate and loving cat. That Siamese cat was a very jealous cat and a strongly annoying entity in the house. He adored only his master. When Regular Bean was not at home, the cat was lying on a dark carpet in the living room, putting an abundance of his white wool there. And then he deliberately did all his "needs" right on the floor in order to annoy Alena and make her clean it again. In the evening he was waiting for the owner outside the house. Seeing his car approaching, he rushed towards him with the joy of a devoted friend. And then the cat jumped into his lap, sat there all evening, hissing and making sure no one came close. In addition, this cat had the habit of sleeping on the owner's bed. And Alena was allergic to the cat's fir. So, from the first day she simply did not have a place there. This cat was like "a domestic terrorist". He seemed fiercely hated a new woman. If Alena took him out of the master bedroom for the night, he sat under the door and meowed so loudly and prolonged that it was impossible to fall asleep. When Alena would go to the toilet, the cat immediately jumped onto the bed. After a few days, Alena gave up. She did not have any strength to fight with Regular Bean's beloved cat. In addition to that, Regular Bean had several unforgivable flaws. It soon became clear that he had a little sexual abilities, and little need for sex. But worst of all, Bob snored terribly. This loud, endless snoring did not give Alena rest for a single minute. If she shoved him lightly, then he was terribly angry. The sleepless nights intensified her irritability and depression. So, in a week, she was forced to move to the next room, where it was a little bit quieter.

In addition, for a long time she could not figure out the names of the buttons on the washing machine, microwave, dishwasher, and other household appliances. She did a little washing, cleaning and cooking for a man who did not express any gratitude to her, taking this for granted.

Eventually Alena concluded that Regular Bean had an empty pocket, had no regular income and no stable work. Barely making ends meet, for his next adventure in Russia he borrowed money from his brother Dan. From time to time, he still worked as a sound engineer on various television channels. In prolonged pauses he spent a lot of time with the phone, calling up different channels, asking for contracts, or driving to distant studios and signing up for any small job a month in advance.

Regular Bean always tried to rent a smaller house and closer to the next job. Most of the money went to gasoline, and to pay the alimony of his last Russian wife number seven. But all the various details of his real life Alena learned too late, when she already lived in his house.

One day he drove Alena to a store, where at the checkout counter at the exit she saw a small bundle of colorful sparkles. Since childhood, Alena was attracted by bright colors. In the poor 1950s, when she grew up with her grandmother in a small, dark house, she did not have toys. This bright tinsel was very cheap, only a few cents. Alena wanted to buy them for her little granddaughter, who still lived in Russia. These sparkles in the form of funny animals seemed to her just some miracle. She dreamed how it would be fun for her daughter and granddaughter to open her letter and be surprised when suddenly these charming spangles in the form of golden, fantastic rain sprinkled on the floor. But Regular Bean, seeing that she put this small bundle in front of the cash register, immediately pushed it away, saying: "You can't buy whatever you want. I have no money for it. "

Alena was simply shocked by such pettiness and this unexpected comment. And she was ashamed in front of the saleswoman for his cheap, stingy statement that hurt her feelings. She felt undeservedly and publicly humiliated. After that, Alena seriously thought that she would not even consider any future with such person. Soon, several other examples convinced her that she would not stay with him for long.

Alena often found colorful magazines in the mailbox. The magazines were an incredible, free and interesting surprise. In Russia she never got anything for free. When she received these colorful fashion magazines, she (like any woman) wanted to buy something. But she adhered to the old rule: "We are not so rich as to buy cheap things." But once she could not resist and decided to show Regular Bean the beautiful photographs of the dresses she dreamed about. He angrily cried out that "there is nowhere to wear such dresses, and there is no need for them."

Alena has always been an independent person, and wanted to stay that way. On the one hand, it seemed stupid to worry about clothes. She had some excellent Parisian outfits with her. But on the other hand, she was very upset by the humiliating dependence on the insignificant man, whom she called "Regular Bean". And then one day, she decided to buy herself something without his knowledge, with her own money, about which he did not know yet. But Regular Bean busy with his own affairs did not pay attention to Alena's appearance at all. The new purchase went unnoticed.

But the most humiliating for Alena was Regular Bean's handouts in the form of twenty dollars a month for her "pocket money" for lunch. This was another example of the ugliness of his miserable material condition and his life. Alena laughed at him to herself, but it was a laugh through her tears. After the incident with glittering and the photos of the beautiful dresses, she did not want to run into new hot-tempered anger or gross scandal with Regular Bean again. At that time, she tried not to aggravate the situation with her arguments.

***

Long time ago, Alena's grandma told her: "Choose a husband by his character, but not by his pretty face. You will live not with a face, but with a character." Soon, Alena began to better understand English. Knowing that the past is the key to the present, she tried to ask Regular Bean about his past, childhood and his parents. It was then that it became clear that as a child his personality was indelibly damaged. He was mortally afraid of his tyrannical father, who did not allow any objections to his will, and beat the boy for the slightest disobedience. In addition, Regular Bean deeply hated his selfish mother. He always spoke negatively about her, blaming her for greed and smoking and rejecting him as a child. A man who did not have a good relationship with his mother will never be a very good husband. The hatred towards his mother, in the end, turned into hidden hostility to any woman next to him. The problems of his childhood passed on to his attitude, and were aggravated by the influence of his previous failed marriages. Although, apparently, he still wanted to have female participation and warmth.

A cold wall of estrangement and misunderstanding lay between them. He could not keep any of his seven marriages with Russian women. But every time, he wished to prove that all previous women were not good enough for him, or that he made a mistake choosing them. He did not see that all his problems and misfortunes were hidden inside him. His passion for pornography and flirting on the computer replaced his communication with a real woman. He was not able to make an effort, or did not want to give up old habits, and could not build a relationship with a woman living nearby.

His last Russian wife (after getting her Green Card) was unable to bear the poverty and neglect of Regular Bean, and filed for divorce. Regular Bean had to pay her alimony for the next ten years, because he pulled her out of her comfortable Moscow life. Moreover, Regular Bean periodically locked himself in his room while talking on the phone with women from his past. In addition, he made new acquaintances on the Internet. Interest in other women, phone sex, and viewing pornographic pictures in magazines was a sign of an empty soul and a sick psyche. Such a man did not have good prospects for happiness with any real woman.

Day by day, Alena discovered many different problems that she could not tolerate. For example, he did not have the habit of taking off shoes when entering the house. He always walked around the house in the same shoes that he wore all day. Then he would sit on the sofa in front of the TV, setting his feet (with shoes) on the coffee table. Alena, who loved cleanliness, was very upset. The concept of personal hygiene in Regular Bean was in last place. He did not have the habit of washing his hands. Arriving home at night, he immediately grabbed his cat, and went directly to the refrigerator. Without closing the refrigerator door, he clutched at the pan, and stuffed into his mouth everything that came across there. Alena advised him that "it would be good to wash your hands first". In reply, he roughly barked back that it didn't concern her, and he would leave the germs wherever he wanted in his house.

On top of everything, his wardrobe consisted of only five or six cheap and monotonous T-shirts and a pair of jeans. He scattered everywhere his well-worn shirts and socks, which he did not like to wash. Of course, he did not have good cologne or face lotion, because these were extra expenses in his meager budget. His toenails and arms always had a black line of dirt.

Regular Bean was very proud that he had two cars. One was a Ford, and the other one was an old, beaten truck, in which he went to his work. Soon, relative of Regular Bean convinced him that Alena should get her California driver's license, and start attending English courses. Regular Bean suggested she would take a bus to get there. But the buses ran around town occasionally, and only on certain routes.

In spite of everything, gritting her teeth, pinching her pride into a fist, crying alone, Alena tried to please him and persuade him to get married quickly. The day came when Alena was able to beg Regular Bean to go to Nevada for two days and register a marriage without delay. Registration of the marriage was carried out hastily in some simple cheap office. During the ceremony, Alena repeated after the official man some words completely incomprehensible to her and got her marriage license. It was that thing, in the name of which Alena sacrificed her well-being in her homeland. The case to which she went for a very long time was done: she was married to an American.

One day, Regular Bean found out that Alena brought with her from Russia a huge (according to his concepts) amount of money. A month after her arrival, without the knowledge of Regular Bean, his brother Dan helped her to open a bank account. Alena put her money there for safety. But one day Dan told his brother - Regular Bean - about her money in his bank. One day, Alena asked Regular Bean to give her lunch money, but he immediately rudely told her that she had her own account. And then, he began to insist that she transfer her money to their joint account, where he had only his one hundred dollars. Then, he began to demand more and more that Alena spend her own money on food, gas for his car, and to pay for their rented house. When she answered him the noble men did not do this, he almost cried out in hysteria that she was planning to ruin him, make him bankrupt, and this must be put to an end.

Soon, realizing that he would not be able to get hold of her money, Regular Bean completely ceased to pay attention to Alena. He was angry all the time, and did not talk to her. It was clear that Regular Bean was plotting something. The fear settled in the soul of Alena that did not let her sleep. Fearing the worst, she soon simply transferred the money back to Russia. Now she understood why in Russia Regular Bean chose some wealthy women as his brides.

Daily stress, loneliness, and absolute silence in the house where she lived led Alena into a deep depression. Day by day, she saw less and less sense to stay in a new country and wait for some blessings and miracles. The relationships with this kind of a man could only lead to the usual logical completeness. Alena could not to put up with him. She needed a breath of fresh air. She wanted to be in the familiar atmosphere of her country. She dreamed of relaxing among her family and rethinking her life. Unable to withstand all this turbidity and stress, she soon simply returned to her foggy, rainy St. Petersburg.

When Regular Bean understood that he couldn't get anything out from Alena, he took advantage of her absence and filed for a divorce. And most importantly, he was anxious to start another adventure with the hope of getting rich with the help of a less obstinate foreigner. In any third world country, he could still console his vanity by playing the part of a wealthy American in whom inexperienced women believed. But for Alena it was necessary to start all over again. And fate drew its own, unexpected paths, bringing new amazing turns and events.

Breezing

In June 1996, Alena returned to Russia, collected her daughter and granddaughter, and went to Gelendzhik, to her beloved Black Sea. Alena's native resort town was still the most beautiful place on earth. Her caring and loving grandmother Anna was still alive there, and waited for her to visit.

These two weeks in June were for Alena the most wonderful vacation. Sea air always had a calming effect on her, purging negative energy and all stresses. All worries were dissolved in the waves of the warm sea. It was a great time of rest. In the evenings, they wandered the streets and promenades of the magical town, taking many photos as a keepsake. The main thing was that she was next to her daughter and granddaughter, feeling that no one in the world could be dearer than them. According to Orthodox tradition, they christened Alena's granddaughter Mary in a local church. Then Alena sold her inheritented house, and left Gelendzhik, without knowing that it was forever.

BOOK 3. New Life

Well rested, Alena and her family returned to St. Petersburg. Alena again bought a tourist visa to France, packed her bags, and paid for a hotel in Paris. But just before the trip, she received several letters from the United States. One day, she was traveling with her former son-in-law and daughter to the city center, and she took with her those few new letters. Although she no longer had any desire to return to America and live so far from her family, she nevertheless opened one letter, just for the sake of elementary curiosity.

It was a short letter from a man named Victusha. His name sounded completely Russian and reminded Alena of one of her good childhood friends with the same name. Only her childhood friend Victusha had lived nearby in her distant, beautiful childhood. And only he always was kind and attentive to her. For some reason, suddenly Alena's heart trembled from an amazing and beautiful foreboding. In the letter there was a photo of a handsome man with a simple, friendly face. The stranger's pleasant appearance and his kind smile radiated warmth. From the photo came something very dear and understandable, which immediately conquered Alena. Also, she saw on the photo a seascape that pinched her soul. The man stood against the backdrop of the well-recognized cliffs of the coastline of her beloved Black Sea. There was a strange, but clear feeling that this photo was another connecting thread sent to her by the fates.

In addition to a wonderful photo of a pleasant man, and a lovely name, the letter also struck Alena. It was printed on a computer in a laconic style, with no embellishments. Also, it was striking in its sincerity, logic and efficiency. The letter sounded simple and clear, like a good business plan. Victusha clearly and point by point listed what exactly he wants to find in his future wife, and why he wants to meet a Russian woman. It was very concrete, and therefore commanded Alena's attention. To everything else, he assured her of his sincere help and support if she decided to come to him. After all the previous ordeals, for Alena the promise of help was decisive. It sounded completely new and immediately attracted her a lot. Alena was sure that she finally met a real knight man who does not plan to profit or live at her expense. And she went to Paris with the desire to write to Victusha from there. Alena wanted to ask him to fly there, or to clarify with him how he plans their meeting in America.

***

The New Year 1996 in Paris ended. But Alena had several wonderful letters from Victusha, and decided to once again try her luck in the United States. When she arrived at the Paris De Gaulle Airport, she suddenly found out that her paid return ticket to America was canceled. She immediately realized that this was done by Regular Bean, who with all his might was trying to create problems for her return. Alena was indignant at such a turn of affairs - the possibility of losing her own money. She strongly expressed her bewilderment to the airport employees. This time she was lucky again. Her place in the airplane has not yet been sold, and she got on her plane.

During a long flight, Alena thought about her life, family and loving friends. She was a very sensitive person, and also noticed what other people feel and think about. Alena kept optimism and love of life all her life. She always set goals and achieved them. Finding beauty in people was a prerequisite for Alena's good mood. She was a cheerful person by nature, had a good sense of humor, and wanted an easy relationship. Everywhere she went, all over the world, she made friends. They told her that Alena inspired them, and communication with her brings them joy. She needed a smart, romantic gentleman who deserved her trust and would support her in everything. The main thing was that he would be kind and faithful to her, without looking at other women.

She did not want to again send vengeful, destructive energy towards her tormentor, punishing him for the pain and tears that he caused her. She knew that she had this special gift, transmitted to her by the ancient ancestors and sorcerers of Hellas. More than once in the past, Alena used power to punish the one who inflicted a wound on her. From such strong stream of a special energy, her offender soon became ill or had serious troubles. But this incredible force sent to punish someone had, at the same time, undermined Alena's own strength. Over time she became more cautious in using this secret power she had.

***

Once, in her childhood, Alena was struck by a refreshing thought. She came to the conclusion that TIME can be strongly compressed in memory. Then, she could travel through different centuries and the farthest points of the earth. That discovery was just very enjoyable. Then, in one fine day, Alena realized that there was nothing accidental in life. The most incredible events occurred because they had long roots in the past. In some mysterious way, the ends of these threads connected in the present. Alena had examples of secret threads that connected many events of the past a few decades later. Even more striking things happened. Some events, as Alena discovered, began in the nineteenth century, and came to their logical conclusion a hundred years later. Here is how it was.

As Alena learned much later, the new American man from a letter, Victusha had a very smart grandfather. His grandfather was a very good businessman, who was looking for the best ways to increase his capital. In 1913, the Russian economy was one of the strongest in the world, and Russia ranked fifth in terms of its development. The most reasonable at that time was (as Victusha's great-grandfather believed) to invest in one of the most economically powerful states. He wanted to put money in the new achievements which were developing there. Therefore, he bought bonds of Russian railway companies, and also invested in oil companies of the Russian imperial court. Thus, he acted regularly since 1898, buying other bonds in 1903, 1906 and 1911 and in 1915. Of course, in the end, according to his calculations, he planned to get rich enormously. He would be right, and it would have happened. However, the Russian Bolshevik revolution of 1917 had prevented this. The Bolshevik revolution destroyed the centuries-old outstanding achievements of the Russian emperors. At that crucial time, no one could have imagined that after the revolution all members of the royal family would be shot, and factories and enterprises would be nationalized. All foreign securities and bonds were worth nothing more. So, their investors lost everything that they invested in. Fortunately, Victusha's great-grandfather, was a cautious person, and he never took much risk. Therefore, his financial losses in Russia were not as tragic as the events of that time that took place there.

Alena found these bonds in the basement of Victusha's house. For her, this was a big and unexpected surprise, a logical coincidence of Victusha's interests in Russia. As she found out later, in 1994, just two years before her meeting with him, Victusha and a group of farmers were invited to the Crimea. The Russian government suggested that they could help them improve Russian agriculture there. They did not need the advice or experience of American farmers, because they could not use it in the sharply differing climatic and social conditions of Russia. They just needed foreign investment, or at least the supply of new tractors and other equipment. Although this mission was not successful for Crimea, it laid the foundation for Victusha's interest in Russia. Later, it led to an improvement in his life. Fate is ruled in mysterious ways.

When Alena found old Russian bonds, she ordered frames for them and hung them in her husband's office. It was a memory of some existing but invisible and mysterious connections they had. These documents contained secret and very strong threads of the past. At that time, Alena thought that this could be some kind of mystical explanation of why Victusha was interested in rich Russian culture, and finally found her, his great love and wife. So Alena began to unwind this ball of memory, recalling her childhood, and writing books about it. Then it became clearer to understand how these strange mystical threads brought her from one part of the planet to another.

***

Carousel

In 1995, a year before the first meeting of Alena and Victusha, his spoiled wife (her name in Russian sounded like a "Rat"), who wanted to control everything, filed for divorce. At first, it was her next blackmail and measure of intimidation. She threatened Victusha with a divorce if he did not build a stable for her horses. Later, Victusha described that they lived for thirty-three year under the same painful situation. Having a soft, non-conflicting character, for a long time he tried to establish a crumbling relationship with his wife, and even went with her to consult with a psychoanalyst. But in everyday life she was rude and demanding, was not shy in expressions, insulted and humiliated Victusha. Often wild scenes escalated into long scandals, and sometimes she did not disdain the assault. Intolerance grew into the hatred. The former Mexican housekeeper Dora, who worked at Victusha's kiosk, once said to Alena. "They haven't talked for weeks. The house always had a tense atmosphere and unbearably heavy, impenetrable silence. It was the house of the dead. "

Once, the lonely and long unhappy Victusha saw in one of the magazines a photograph of Alena shining with joy. He saw his dream woman, and could not resist the bright and cheerful appearance of Alena. He kept this radiant happiness of the photo, and enjoyed it in the hours of sadness.

Alena at that time planned to stay living in Paris. But Victusha sent her several Fax at the Paris hotel, insisting on a meeting, and promising all kinds of help. But she did not know anything about that man and decided that she would go to him to have fun in that summer without serious obligations. She had already a tourist visa which allowed repeated entries to his country. After a little thought, Alena agreed to meet him in LA. In addition, she had to pick up her personal belongings left in the house of Regular Bean.

Victusha had long craved love and attention. And for the first time in his life, he began to really and passionately dream of meeting that beautiful woman whose wonderful photo he saw in a magazine. He decided that she was the one, and sent his letter to her. This photograph with the image of a charming woman with shining eyes forever remained in his heart. She was a symbol of high, eternal and happy love, which can be found only once in a lifetime.

"How will I recognize you in the airport of LA?" Alena asked him in one of her messages.

"I will be wearing a cowboy hat," he replied, apparently believing that she knew from Hollywood films what a cowboy hat looks like.

***

Arriving in Los Angeles, Alena for a long time could not pass immigration control. Frightened of her return, Regular Bean made a complaint to the immigration service. But all her documents were in order, and she finally received permission to continue the journey, and went to the exit. At that time, obsessed with his dream and distinguished by incredible endurance, Victusha stubbornly waited for Alena for seven hours. When she went upstairs, from afar she saw only one man in a huge hat. She went up to him and said: "Hello. I'm Alena". And he replied: "Nice to meet you. Let's go." And so they began their journey.

Sneaking a glance at the stranger, Alena joyfully noted his average height, slim figure and narrow hips. In addition, he was deliberately, neatly and cleanly dressed in nice gray trousers and a shirt. It was pleasant to note that he was not wearing a cheap T-shirt or shabby jeans, which she could not stand. "His clothing is a polite sign of his respect for our meeting," joyfully thought Alena.

Victusha was only fifty-five years old, and Alena was forty-one. With good compatibility of characters, it was the perfect age difference for a successful marriage. A small mustache and still thick silver-gray hair brought a touch of nobility in his appearance. But a low forehead, excessive wrinkles over the eyelids and glasses closed his eyes. So, Alena could not look into the eyes to unravel his soul. When Victor did not smile, he looked very upset or gloomy. Past troubles experienced, work on the fields, and a difficult marriage made him old early. Many deep wrinkles, especially in the corners of the mouth, gave his face a special severity. Rather thin lips and a small chin spoke of a fickle character. Something in him was too sad, and even tough, which somewhat alerted Alena. But when he smiled, his face became very pleasant, and she wanted to trust him.

Immersed in his thoughts, Victusha was strangely silent all the way. He did not ask about anything, did not seek to immediately learn more about the new girl. He made no effort for polite questions about how her long road went or how she felt. "Either he does not have the experience of a small talk, or does not know how to talk with an exotic stranger, or he is very embarrassed," with concern thought Alena.

Victusha drove his Mercedes smoothly, without overtaking anyone, and carefully following the busy traffic on a wide highway. This was important to note, and spoke of the stability of his character. Tired of a long flight, Alena also did not ask him anything, although she was worried about where they were going and what they would do. It was strange that from the very first moment she simply trusted this unusual person. She now liked him even more than when she saw his first photo.

It is interesting that the first mechanical carousels appeared in Europe in the 18th century, and Peter the Great brought one of these attractions to Russia. Carousels were very popular among young nobles. Young people mounted wooden horses or chariots circling around a wooden pillar. They tried during the movement to remove the suspended rings with spears and hit various targets. It was quite active entertainment, in contrast to similar attractions of the late XIX century. Over time, the military orientation of the attraction has become a thing of the past, and it has become popular at fairs.

People on an old carousel tried to get a ring from a stick that hung to the right of the carousel. This had to be done very carefully, otherwise you could fall off the horse, and there would be no second chance. No one could get to this ring and take it, because it was extremely difficult. Victusha once said that his magical meeting with Alena reminded him of a fabulous story of a carousel. He made a very strong effort, reached out and got it.

***

From the first instant, Alena and Victusha felt that they had been looking for each other all their lives. Finally, fate brought them together. Victusha, having met his dream, and having received even more than he expected, was afraid to frighten off his luck. He did not want, and was not able to separate for a single day from his beloved woman, who became for him the whole meaning of life.

From the airport, they drove to the house of his parents, who were then on a cruise in Europe. The house was located in the beautiful, old town of Tustin, where Victusha had spent his childhood. The house was large and beautiful, with nice furniture and expensive carpets. The interior, decoration, the whole situation in it reminded Alena of her mother's house in Gelendzhik, and how she once lived. She immediately calmed down. She understood that she would not need to humiliate herself because of the stinginess and greed of a man or begging in a new country.

A few days later, Victusha settled Alena closer to his estate, in a small cozy "Resort". The mountains surrounding the resort resembled the Gelendzhik ranges. It was a good sign and comforting for Alena. They swam in the resort's pool and enjoyed the surrounding nature. Alena admired Victusha's slender figure, and tried not to pay attention to the frequent sullenness of his face. The stern expression on his face did not concern her personally, but was directed inside his sad thoughts and the situation in his house. When he looked at Alena, his whole appearance was getting much younger. He tried to square his shoulders, as if he wanted to be stronger and more confident in everything. His eyes shone with joy in response, meeting her smile. It was evident that Victusha simply enjoyed all the happiness that fate had sent him. He swam not only in the pool, but also in his unexpectedly strong emotions overwhelming him.

Almost immediately reaching for Alena in return trust, Victusha felt the need to constantly talk with her about his past. Long years of painful relations with his ex-wife, her endless demands and insults, had left deep wounds in his heart. Victusha needed to talk with a sincere, sensitive person. With tears in his eyes, he shared with Alena, his gentle stranger all his sorrows. But due to poor knowledge of English, Alena did not understand even half of what he was talking about. But, seeing his pain, she listened with deep attention and empathy. She herself experienced many sorrows and pains in her life, understood his emotions, and was sincerely sorry for the good man. In Russian women, pity often develops into love. The pity is always on the verge with the ability to love a person who is sorry for.

But even more important in this nascent relationship was that he also listened very carefully to everything that Alena was trying to tell him. Victusha, too, seemed to understand Alena at a glance. Such attention from a man was new, incredibly pleasant and strengthened her respect and

106

craving for him. Respect is always the foundation of a deep relationship.

Alena already had lived a long life with many tragedies and had enormous experience of several failed marriages. She was afraid that the difficult experience of the past also left an indelible mark on Victusha's soul and mutilated his character. She had strong fears that he would transfer his negative feelings of his past (out of habit) to their new relationships. Most of all, Alena was afraid to be in the center of a meat grinder of his former family, whose negativity could spoil their love and life. She counted on his love only. Only his love could save them.

***

Spying

Before leaving for America, Alena had several plastic surgeries and looked incredibly young. Moreover, from the many unexpected, generous gifts and pleasant surprises of Victusha, she was all delighted with happiness. The wonderful resort town where Victusha settled her for a few days was very pleasant, and she dreamed of staying there as long as possible. Alena felt a rare, carefree state of complete relaxation, and did not care about anything, completely trusting Victusha. Soon he put her in a hotel, settling across from his ranch. Checking in at this tiny hotel, he introduced Alena as his wife. But, having paid for the number, he forgot his credit card at the reception. The hotel clerk was surprised that his client lives very close, opposite the hotel. And wishing to please him, the next day he sent a clerk with this credit card to Victusha's home. But at that moment he was not there, and the clerk gave the credit card to his ex-wife, who still lived there. Although she was the one who started the divorce one year before it. But this time, she got especially alarmed. Still having Victusha's financial resources and access to his bank accounts, she hired a private investigator to keep track of the "sweet couple".

The private detectives were husband and wife. From that moment they followed Victusha and Alena for their every step. They took photos of the happy lovers everywhere, as "the evidence of Victusha's infidelity and to prove that he has an adventurous nature." Alena saw that they were being photographed stealthily. But she naively thought that people simply admire their carefree happiness. Once, seizing the moment when Victusha was not around, that wrinkled old woman-detective approached Alena and said with hatred: "I don't understand how you can be with such an old man. He's twice your age. How can you break up a family! "

Alena did not know the whole background of the events happening behind her back. She was shocked by the injustice of such a conclusion. It sounded wild from a complete stranger. Alena turned pale, could not breathe and momentarily lost consciousness. She could neither speak nor smile habitually. It was like in a scary movie. But then Victusha returned, shining with happiness. She saw his loving face, and did not dare to tell about the gross insult inflicted. They simply continued their joyful journey.

***

Visists

When Victusha's parents returned from the European cruise, he, as a noble man with serious intentions, decided to introduce them to Alena. She was delighted, because, it seemed, it was a good sign. But in the house of his imperious mother, during lunch, there was an unpleasant tension at the table. In the presence of a tough father, Victusha looked like he was lost, was gloomy silent, finding no words. It seemed that he was either afraid of his powerful parents, or felt some kind of guilt. In their presence, he was not a confident person, no matter how Alena wanted to see him.

From childhood, Victusha considered his clever, energetic mother and powerful father to be the indisputable authority. In addition, since his youth, he felt deep guilt before his parents. This agonizing feeling lived in Victusha's soul from the time when he decided, under the influence of his friend, to illegally transport a woman across the border of two Germanys. Victusha's soul was tormented with shame for his rash act and the loss of someone else's car. His sense of fear of doing something wrong or accidently offending someone always prevented him both in life and in business. This fear deprived him of firmness, independence and confidence of his actions. This is why Victusha more often followed persistent persuasion and the advice of others. Making some decisions under the influence of more powerful personalities, later Victusha regretted about losing a lot, but could not fix it.

After college, he served the army, then, got married, becoming an obedient husband for thirty-three years. At the same time, he worked on the ranch under the guidance of his strict and severe father. When they met, Alena saw that Victusha somehow depended too much on his parents. Also, at that time, not only his personal life but his business was in decline. A man must make business decisions in a sober mind and a calm state of mind. However, Victusha already for more than a year was under great stress from the problems with his ex-wife, her endless demands and the divorce.

At that famous first lunch at his parents' house, Alena felt the tension between them. But she was happy about her relationships with Victusha, and didn't feel any guilt before his parents. Also, according to European customs, being silent at the table in a company was the greatest rudeness. A polite conversation was an integral part of any feast. Beside it could be a skillful pleasure, it is also a chance to get to know each other better. Outgoing and polite Alena, slightly embarrassed by her weak knowledge of English and a strong accent, was afraid to speak first. But then she thought that they all here did not know any languages at all except English. Also, she knew that talking about religion, politics and money in America was considered bad form. And therefore, the theme of travel seemed to her safe and enjoyable for any person and was attractive to any society. She especially wanted to talk about her favorite Leningrad, one of the most beautiful cities in the world.

For more than ten years she worked as a guide in many museums there, and knew this great city well. On every street there was an architectural masterpiece, described in many books and glorified by composers and poets. Finally, she decided to help to "melt the ice" of the tense silence of the table. Showing her good upbringing, she asked in a friendly and a cheerful way: "Did you like St. Petersburg?"

Maybe her question was not formulated correctly. But she expected everyone to be delighted with this help and having a neutral topic to talk about, and immediately try to smooth out the unpleasant atmosphere. To her surprise, unexpectedly and sharply, Victusha's father answered disrespectfully, as he chopped off: "No." And he fell silent again, staring at his plate, as everybody else. Then, in a minute, realizing that this was the height of hostility and rudeness, Victusha's mother added, as if making excuses: "It was raining all the time, it was cold, and Ed caught a cold." That hostility of his parent never was changed.

***

When Alena came to the USA, she thought, that everybody spoke perfect English without any accents. She did not know that America was a "melting pot" of different cultures and languages, and that in each State people speak with a different accent. California, once owned by Mexico and having a border with it, is crammed with Mexicans. Basically, they work in low-paying jobs and in maintenance staff. Victusha spoke Spanish language with his workers on his ranch. Alena also began to learn Spanish.

Alena and Victusha were very happy when they were left alone, without his relatives. But Victusha had a large family, and his mother often convened family meetings, insisting that everyone there flawlessly appear.

His mother also invited all members of the family to some society events. It was clear that the honest Victusha did not plan to hide his Alena from anyone, and he wanted to go to any celebration with her.

One day, at a rich party, in a huge room among a crowd of strangers, beautifully dressed up Alena felt like a defenseless kid. She wanted to be seen and included in the conversation. But she did not see Victusha anywhere. So, she went to a group of people, where his father stood with other people. In the pause that appeared, the easiest way was to resume the conversation with a short remark about the weather. So, she did. But in response, without even listening to her, Victusha's father turned around sharply and loudly declared as he chopped off: "It's embarrassing to speak English so badly."

Everyone around was embarrassed, not even finding a joke, to smooth over the impending awkward silence. From this undeserved insult, Alena all contracted and blushed. By the nature, she was proud, adamant, did not let anyone offend her. Knowing her own virtues, she never tolerated anyone's superiority over herself. Her deep self-respect was something what raised her independence and helped her to survive in Russia.

At that moment of a new public insult, she did not think that political propaganda could be behind it, or many people might have stereotypes about what a woman from poor Russia should be like. But she was simply very hurt, stood alone, and was extremely uncomfortable. At this party, from an incredibly gross public insult, an uncontrollable fire of revenge suddenly boiled inside Alena again. She immediately wanted to blur out, if her future father-in-law knew at least one other language. But she once already promised herself not to answer anybody at their level. She tried to hide her eyes sparkling with anger. Not wanting to quarrel with the old man, she quietly went into the crowd of strangers, looking for Victusha for comfort. His love was the best restraining force and protection.

From the first day, unexpectedly meeting an unreasonable cold attitude from the relatives of her fiancé, Alena was very upset. She lost her parents early, and her cherished dream was to find a new family in her marriage. From an early age, she knew that there was no one to protect her. She had learned to defend herself early, was sharp on the tongue, and quick in revenge. Life circumstances taught her to defend herself, to answer the blow with an even stronger blow, or hide and take revenge when the enemy does not expect it. She did not understand Christ's wisdom about non-resistance to evil by violence. She did not understand why she should turn the other cheek to the new punch. Very early in her life, Alena understood that if one day she allowed her own humiliation, then people would continue to insult her, push her around and make her obey their will. On her street where she grew up, Alena saw such humiliated and beaten children who were always at the beck and call of the stronger leaders. She herself grew up a leader, not wanting to obey anyone, and always fought to the victorious end, even with those who were older and stronger.

In adolescence, unexpected rudeness and unjustified insult brought Alena into a tailspin, and she was lost. A little later, she learned to recover a little faster from this paralyzing shock, an unjust insult and hurt pride. Once she internally decided that if only she could ignore the insult and not notice the rude person, it will be much better for her. She began to console herself that if she would be answering the rude insults it would mean that she believes in them. But she valued herself highly. But to be silent in the answer to the insults took all her strength. She was a fighter, and never mastered those skills.

At the moment of insult, she always felt that in her soul instantly flashed and raged an uncontrollable, growling, fiery beast, ready to tear to pieces the offenders. Often Alena could not even control it, and he crumbled everything in his path. But sometimes the insults came from relatives. In that case, she was afraid to use the destructive power of her energy against them. Then, she learned to simply shut herself in, fencing off these people with everything she could (most often with a wall of intolerable silence). However, most often with strangers she mentally, at the moment

112

of resentment and insult, sent the offender a strong impulse of destructive energy. This huge clot of terrible power immediately settled in a weak area of the body of her enemy, gradually killing him with various ailments.

Once, a ninety-five-year-old grandmother told Alena the secret of her birth, and spoke about a very strange property that she owned and should be careful about how to use it. That power was passed on to her from the women of their ancient Greek family. It was transmitted only from grandmother to the grandchildren. Alena then wondered how and when it would be best to warn her own granddaughter of this inner, all-conquering power.

***

At that time, the man in love apparently did not think at all what they would do with the new woman and how to live. Victusha was adrift, living one day at a time. His ex-wife, after she has learned about his hot romance and travels with Alena, began struggling to delay the final divorce. Her goal was to punish Victusha, to make him suffer even more, to draw huge amounts out of him, not agreeing to any reasonable conditions. And Victusha, who finally decided to radically change his life, wanted to introduce Alena to his relatives, hoping for their support.

When people live together, they build relationships not only with each other, but also with everybody around. Friends, children, and relatives can influence a couple's relationship, both positively and negatively. Already during the early period, the main thing to understand is how he treats his precious "soul mate" among strangers.

For a woman, the most important thing is to feel her exclusivity. The most important measure of his attitude will be how he emphasizes the significance of his relationships with a woman in the society. Only that will be the guarantee of the future happiness. There is no way around it.

***

One day Victusha decided to introduce her to his relatives. With the enthusiasm, Alena and Victusha set off on a short trip through California.

Their first stop was at the magnificent estate of his younger brother Petin. Brother Petin was a very friendly, polite and hospitable person. He never got divorced, did not divided his property. So, he was rich, and seemed very happy. All his life he was married to one woman whom he loved very much and was ready to forgive her all her whims. His wife Nona had emigrated from a foreign county with her parents when she was a child. Then she tried very hard to become a "real" American. Her character was typical of sly women, accustomed to intrigue. Having successfully married, she got into a chic atmosphere, which she always dreamed of. The versatile connections and prestige of her husband's family opened the way to high society, where she sought to reign. Her goal was by all means to achieve even greater prosperity, by obtaining a good inheritance for her children. In order to achieve that and the exceptional attention and love of her rich mother in law, she needed to eliminate the influence of other women in the family. She devoted all her life to this goal, and taught her husband and children how to do that. At the end, she got it all, as she wanted.

Suddenly meeting Victusha and Alena in her house, she politely greeted them, but then tried to exclude her presence next to the guests. There was nothing to do there, among fields and plantations. So, while feeling cold and alienated, Alena and Victusha spent only one night with them. To Alena's great surprise, when leaving Victusha left one hundred dollars on the table of his brother's office. Alena was slightly puzzled by the strange reception of Nona. "Apparently, the money is more important here than kinship," she thought. Later, Nona continued to make excuses to other relatives for the fact that she sheltered Victusha and Alena in her house for one night. On all meeting of some family celebrations, she usually told people that Victusha misled her. "He said he would come to us with the girls. I thought he would bring his daughters." So this is how she explained to everyone in a row her oversight, having provided "hospitality" to officially unmarried couple.

***

The next stop was at house of his middle brother, Jim. Alena was also surprised by his pleasant house. It became clear that this sibling as also a rather wealthy man. Jim's face also expressed kindness and agreeable personality. But he looked somehow not very happy, and not well groomed, although he tried to seem cheerful. He was a twin with Victusha's sister Berta. Berta lived in a different State, and has been several times unsuccessfully married. Not too long ago, Jim also experienced a difficult divorce. His ex-wife was incredibly aggressive, pragmatic, grip and prudent woman. She quickly managed to grab the oil mines from him, as well as all his shares in a very profitable business. He had been dating the same woman for ten years, and could not find any strength for a new marriage to that grasping woman. Her name also sounded like a "Rat", if we translate it in Russian. And observing her later, Alena got prove and finally believed that the name transfers all the characteristics of this animal. It also means "the traitor". It was not far from the reality of her character. She was a tall, awkward but overbearing nurse. Any work always leaves its mark on a person. So this woman was used to imperiously commanding the sick, and indeed everyone around, including the good Jim. At first Alena was confused and dumbfounded by the shameless, sexual frankness of this rude woman. It looked like this "Rat" was not indifferent to Victusha. She behaved very aggressively and obviously flirted with him, as if Alena was not at all around. It seemed that the "Rats" lived with Victusha's brother only because they were unusually similar to each other, like two drops of water.

One day, unable to stop the harassment towards her man, Alena pointed it out to Victusha, and told him about her concerns about the immoral behavior of a crazy woman. Alena emphasized that only the "street professionals" kiss on the lips with the other's man. But Victusha never believed in anything bad around him. He generally had the habit of explaining everything on the positive side, seeing the world in "pink glasses", and endowing everyone around with his own noble qualities. And this time, he explained the behavior of the "Rat" by their "kindred" and "friendly" relations. As Alena soon learned, it was in his character to get along with everyone around him, even to the detriment of his relationship with his own wife.

In time, Alena became convinced that "Rat" were jealous, envied and competed with her for Victusha's attention. At all family meetings, she tried her best to be near to Victusha for family photo, and sit next to him at the table, while impatiently asked a lot of questions. She did not care about the feelings of Victusha's brother, her lover. She did not value Jim or their long relationship. Her main point was to distract Victusha from Alena, and put all attention to herself. Her behavior showed a very low level of morality, disrespect and disregard for the person with whom she lived. Jim and Victor, not wanting to aggravate the situation, simply remained silent indifferently. All the others, busy with events and experiences of their own life, did not pay any attention to this. Only Alena stood guard over her relationship with Victusha, and was hurt badly.

The women of the family saw that all their efforts to quarrel and separate Victusha and Alena did not succeed. Day by day, they treated Alena worse and worse. One day, leaving the restaurant, Alena and Victusha walked side by side, holding hands. But "Rat" went faster, caught up with them, and roughly pushing Alena aside, whispered sharply: "Get out of here." Then, she grabbed Victusha's arm, saying "I need to talk to you," while walking and hugging him. She was strong and the same height as Victusha. Alena was not able to fight her, even if she wanted to. In addition, such unjustified aggression on the part of a "family member" simply shocked Alena.

She looked at Victusha, seeking his protection, but he either pretended not to hear, or did not really notice the malicious intent of his brother's mistress. Victusha did not react to this impudent trick of a rude woman. After the family meeting in Hawaii one year before, he considered her his "friend." The naive masculine gender does not know that they cannot have "friends" among women. Each woman looks at any man from the position of the owner, and she is always terribly jealous of his attention to the other woman.

For annual anniversaries, Victusha's wealthy parents had the opportunity to invite a huge number of people. Shortly before the meeting of Alena and Victusha, the whole huge clan of his family was resting on the island of Maui. The most amazing thing was that his parents traditionally paid for all guests their accommodation. Even the most distant relatives and family "friends" began to count on this generosity. So, every year about fifty people gathered for such "family" celebrations. Victusha had already bad situation with his ex-wife, but he did not want to tell anybody about it, and flew to Hawaii alone. There he spent a lot of time with his brothers and their women. And one evening, sitting by the ocean, drinking wine and admiring the sunset, Victusha opened up with his brother's girlfriend about the unpleasant situation of his own life. She took it as a sign of his special attention and sympathy to her. Being a tough predator, this nurse, apparently secretly cherished the hope to get Victusha to herself. And with Jim she was only because he was very similar to Victusha. Further events confirmed her jealousy towards Alena.

***

Jealousy

In 1998 Jim girlfriend Rate insisted that he would marry her officially. She was jealous that Victusha and Alena already got married. Although Jim did not see any need for this, he succumbed to рук persistent persuasion because of his natural softness. Their wedding was in their local church, followed by an incredibly crowded and rich dinner. She tried to make her wedding day more significant than Alena had. After the dinner everybody were invited to spend a night in a special resort nearby paying for that their own money.

Being a very polite person, Victusha saw no reason why he should have avoided his brother's wedding, and they arrived at the wedding feast.

Entering the hall, Alena immediately felt that an atmosphere of intense conspiracy was floating in the air. In connection with the special genes and childhood characteristics, she had an unusually deep intuition, and a sharp mind developed for understanding intrigues. In that evening, all brothers, their wives and parents were sitting at the same table. Soon the dance music began to play. Alena noticed that the women of the family were whispering behind her. Then Victusha's mother dropped the phrase, saying that the men should dance with women. But Victusha's siblings pretended that this did not concern them. Then Nona, the wife of his younger brother, considering herself "the navel of the earth" and the queen of any event, looking at Victusha, and in a demanding tone, declared that she especially loved to dance.

For Alena, the main pleasure always was the opportunity to dance with Victusha, and she longed for any opportunity to do it. At this moment, she had already understood the insidious conspiracy against her. She immediately continued Nona's phrase:

"In this case, you and your husband have to go to dance classes, as we do with Victusha. Let's go dear, to dance! "

Alena and Victusha went to the center of the ballroom to enjoy their favorite dance. After many joint lessons, they did it very synchronously, harmoniously and elegantly. But right after them, the drunken "Rat-bride" pulled to the dance floor the slightly resisting groom Jim. However, there, barely standing on her feet, "Rat-newlywed", immediately left Jim, and staggering walked to the dancing Alena and Victusha.

She easily pushed Alena abruptly to the side by her huge hands. Then, she grabbed Victusha in her tenacious embrace, and hanged on his chest. Alena stood nearby, stunned. She warned Victusha in advance that something scandalous would happen again at this party. At home, this conversation, as always, passed Victusha's ears. He forgot all Alena's warnings. Only here, in the midst of their own dance, finding himself in the tenacious mites of a kind of "relative", Victusha tried to break free. But the Rats held tight to his white jacket. And then she again dug into his lips with a greedy kiss, as if on the rights of a "bride." It was then that Victusha turned out of the sleeves of his jacket, and they went out from this den. But the vengeful "bride" did not calm down, and rushed after them. Not paying any attention to the quiet remarks of her already official husband, she unceremoniously tried to plop down on the sofa between Alena and Victusha. There, even before her arrival, there was no room for an additional person. Then, the polite Alena tried to get up, squeezed from all sides. But Victusha, who had already received his sight, held Alena tightly next to him. He made an effort not to allow the slutty woman to squeeze close by. But she did not let up. Then Victusha and Alena had no choice but to get up together and go away. Early the next morning, having paid their room, they left the hotel without saying a word to anyone. Arriving home, Alena tried to find understanding and trust among Victusha's family members. She wrote about this incident to his sister Bertha, but she did not believe her, responding with condemnation.

***

Each person's life is incredibly valuable and important. Perhaps some famous parents sometimes unintentionally or unconsciously exaggerate the importance of their own lives. At the same time, they can harm the lives of other people, without making any effort to notice or evaluate the achievements of another family member. They may think that their own life is much more interesting, that they are the truly outstanding members of society. At least some events of the new family, where Alena appeared in 1996, led her to these conclusions.

Being an honest, courageous, and very patient man, Victusha hid all his problems and sorrows from his relatives, without telling about the difficult first marriage. None of them knew about his past and an unhappy life with his ex-wife.

And when Alena came into his life, he hoped that he could share with his relatives the happiest time with the new woman. But gradually his hope faded. His relatives, by their behavior and attitude towards Alena, denied Victusha his right to his own decisions, his holy right to happiness.

***

***

Games

At all family gatherings, the jealous women tried to put Alena and Victusha away from each other. Alena noticed this from the very beginning, when one day, they flew to the wedding of Victusha's nephew in Texas. Victusha's sister, absorbed in her own life, was not a sensitive to others. Berta did not think about the psychological state of her brother or about the comfort of his foreign wife. She put Alena away from Victor, in an unfamiliar company of the half deaf old people. Alena felt, that Berta intentionally had a desire to show her "who is who". This time, as well as in the future, she made another effort trying to quarrel Alena and Victusha. A future sister-in-law clearly did not want to recognize Alena as Victusha's bride. Alena found herself surrounded by the strangers, unfriendly and arrogant people. They did not make any effort to talk with her about anything. It created an atmosphere of awkwardness.

This time, Victusha did not find possible or was not able to disobey his younger sister at her home. So, all the dinner he sat on the other side of the table. Alena loved to communicate, make new friends, and always had something interesting to discuss with people. But her strong accent, natural shyness created additional uncertainty, preventing Alena from relaxing or

120

easily communicating with her surroundings. She did not have any friends or supporters of their happiness among Victusha's relatives. Nobody among them ever made her feel more welcoming, comfortable or not as lonely.

At the next gala dinner, Alena noticed again the plot of women against her. But this time, she sneaked into the banquet room in advance. She saw that the cards with their names were indeed very far apart, and she immediately moved them closer. What a surprise was on the faces of the family members when they saw that Victusha and Alena were sitting next to each other. But the evening had already begun. Nobody could openly demand to transfer Alain away from Victusha. They could not do a scandal. And in the future, Alena kept her ears open, and at all banquets changing cards with their names in advance.

But the games went on. Once, Victusha and Alena went to visit his parents for Christmas. In the living room there was a beautiful Christmas tree with a pile of wrapped gifts under it. Alena was really excited to see such feasting atmosphere which was inspiring to her.

All women love unpretentious gifts. Alena well understood that cheap, unnecessary things or souvenirs only offend a woman. In her beloved Paris, there were men who tried to make Alena generous gifts with a hint. However, she most often refused anything meaningless or too expensive from men. She didn't want to feel obligated to a man, who did not intend to make a commitment to her.

After the Christmas dinner in Victusha parents' house, everyone went to the living room, and began to make gifts with all kinds of baubles. When the turn came to Victusha, he, with shining eyes, handed Alena a small black velvet box. Surprised Alena opened it with the trepidation, gasped and froze from her overwhelming feelings. Gold earrings with the diamonds sparkled in the box. It was first diamonds in her life. She did not expect such a valuable gift, and was unable to contain her delight, looking at Victusha with love. Everyone saw her joy and was torn by curiosity, and all their attention was fixed on Alena. Then, Victusha's mother demanded to show everyone what is so amazing there. Seeing the jewel, she hid her eyes and pursed her lips wanting to hide her disappointment and anger. But out of politeness, hiding behind a duty, insignificant phrase, she dryly said: "How sweet".

An awkward silence followed. Another big pile of nameless gifts lay in the center of the room. Then, in order to seize the attention to her again, brother's girlfriend "Rat" energetically suggested playing a game to distribute these gifts. The rules of the game were strange, more suitable for some jerks or for the rednecks. She said that her co-workers played it recently at her work party, and described the game.

The first person in a circle took a gift from the pile, unfolded it, and asked the person sitting next to him, if he wanted to take up this gift for himself. If someone did not like the gift, then he could return it back to the pile on the floor. At the same time, if somebody who loved the gift wanted to keep it, any other person in the room still could steal that gift from a winning person. This game has one condition. According to the rules, it was possible to steal that present from another person only twice. For the third time, the gift was left with the person who wished it last. The bored society enthusiastically agreed to play. Even though, the rules of the game seemed to Alena specifically demonstrate the low moral level of the players. But she could not get up and leave the room,

When the turn came to Alena, the host unfolded a wonderful porcelain vase for cakes, and gave it to Alena. Alena and Victusha already had similar plates, and a vase of the same style would be very handy in their house. But then the jealous "Rat" intercepted this gift for herself. Then, the envious Nona took it from her. Alena felt that they would never let her get something really nice in this game. She pushed Victusha and whispered: "Take this to us, please!"

And Victusha, who finally began to be aware of the unfairness his relatives treated Alena, won back the present for them. This was the third time after which no one could take away this gift from him. An expression of hostility and irritation appeared on the faces of all women in the room. But the rules were dictated by them. There was nothing to do, but only "bite the elbows," which they tried to do all evening. But Alena and Victusha soon left them, and headed to their happy nest to love each other forever.

***

BOOK 4. Elkins

The significant, fateful and mystical meeting of Victusha and Alena forever changed their life. Victusha's behavior, his attention and attitude towards her also turned upside down all Alena's ideas about men. It seemed everything around her was lit by his great love. As Alena thought while looking at the first photo of Victusha, he turned out to be an honest and sincere person. He had a very good education and upbringing. He was well-read, traveled a lot, and had an open, broad and progressive outlook on many things in life. One could safely say that he, too, was "a citizen of the world or a man of the earth." In this they coincided strongly, and it was pleasant. The most important, he had a strong patience, perseverance and desire to overcome all the obstacles to his happiness.

At this time, he still had his new business in Kentucky. He did not expect that his coal mine that he bought recently would be soon doomed to bankruptcy, and for a long time it would be sucking out all his savings. For several years, Victusha did not have the opportunity to get rid of it. But he needed to fly from California to Kentucky every second week to manage all his affairs there.

After unfriendly meetings with his California relatives, Victusha needed to settle with Alena some place where no one knew or disturbed them. They wanted to have some rest in a peaceful surrounding. And one day, he took Alena to Kentucky and settled in a motor home on his coal mine. The climate was very hot with too much humidity. The area was surrounded by jungle and mountains, and pile of dusty black coal. The noise from the machines getting coal from under the ground was intolerable. It was wildness around and she had nowhere to go. Even to reach the most simple and very poor, not high quality store, they drove about one hour. After couples days Alena felt if she was imprisoned or sentenced to hard labor there. Victusha began to think how to improve their lives. But while living there, they began to traveling to different states in his van for weekends. It was fun time getting to know each other and rejoicing in each new day. Alena was completely dissolved in her happiness, Victusha's courtship and in his ardent attention. Unhindered hugs and gentle kisses did not end either day or night.

During these trips Alena realized that each state is different, and people speak with different accents. This gave her some self-confidence. "She was not alone in the USA who had so different pronunciation of English words. Therefore, she should not be so much concerned about this". Step by step, and only thanks to the constant efforts of Victusha and friendly people they met in different states, Alena began to slowly overcome the "cultural shock" of the new country. From time to time, they stopped in a beautiful place, and Alena laid out a picnic in a clearing. After spending a night in their motor home or in hotel, they set off on, rejoicing in freedom and independence.

During the trip, Alena entertained Victusha with her melodic, drawn-out, ancient songs, which her grandmother taught her in childhood. In 1950, it was their only form of entertainment in Russia. There were no karaoke clubs in Russia until the 1990s, and Alena never had no opportunity to sing them to anybody. Victusha was a great music lover and a wonderful listener. Although he did not understand the words of the songs, he rejoiced at their pleasant melody and the tender voice of his beloved woman. Time generously gave them wonderful hours of serenity.

***

Once Alena, to somehow take some free time, decided to ask Victusha about his activities, and did this in the form of an interview. Alena asked him: "As I understand it," she began, "you have been engaged in agriculture all your life in the "SDCounty", where your family has owned land since 1945. Your experience will be interesting to those people who are not related to agriculture.

Victor began his talk. "I grew up on a citrus and avocado ranch in "Or.County." It was a family business. My family also raised livestock, planted vegetables, beans and other crops. I studied at the University of California, where I received a Ph.D. in agricultural economics. After university and two years in the army, I returned to agriculture. My brothers, who live in other parts of California, also took up farming. They have their own plantations of almonds, apples, grapes, barley, carrots, watermelons, etc."

Alena asked: "It looks like you have a lot of family experience. Why did you decide to stay in agriculture?"

Victusha replied: "I grew up on a ranch with a love of nature and the environment. Traditionally, all three generations of my ancestors were engaged in agriculture. My great-grandfather was a beekeeper at O'Neill's Ranch, most of which are now Camp Pendleton and Mission Viejo. My grandfather was a pioneer in citrus cultivation in "OrCounty." My father was one of the first to try avocado production."

Alena asked: How do you perceive your work now?

Victusha replied: "There are too many bureaucratic rules and restrictions imposed in the name of" environmental protection." They make it difficult to work and stay in this business. Often regulations do little to protect the environment. They are the result of the desire of people who do not know anything about agriculture to regulate our activities. Many farmers spend a lot of useless time in political battles, only to get the opportunity to continue to do what they love so much for society - agriculture. I am pessimistic about the future of agriculture.

Alena asked: Please tell us about your favorite and unpleasant parts of your work.

Victusha replied: "My least favorite part of the job is to write the reports required by the government. These are statistics on the production, use of fertilizers, chemicals and a tax report. None of them are attractive, and most are useless. I try to minimize the time spent on these tasks due to the widespread use of my computer. But most of all I enjoy working in the air, on the ground. This may be planting vegetables, trees or working on a tractor. Walking through the plantations it is pleasant to inhale the smell of freshly turned land or flowering trees. In the spring, any work is accompanied by a very delicate smell of orange flowers. In huge quantities, they give the strong effect of rare spirits. Some brides even order such special bouquets of orange flowers for their wedding ceremony. Harvest and the smell of flowering orange trees creates a feeling of happiness and the sense of working on the ground. "

Alena asked: Tell us about the bad or good experience in your work?

Victusha said: "Bad and good experience is really in some way combined. During major floods several years ago, we lost many trees adjacent to the San Luis Rey River. A good aspect of this was that my workers tried to help save the trees. This wonderful feeling of working together in a critical or dangerous situation will remain in my memory for a long time."

Alena asked: Do you have specific responsibilities, complex or difficult aspects?

Victusha: "My job is to understand what needs to be done today and explain it to people who work for me. And then make sure that this is done ("management"). As for what is the most difficult, it would be generally accepted that farmers are dominated by the weather. However, I believe that in today's environment we are dominated by bureaucrats. It is a universally recognized fact that if all normative acts were implemented and put into effect in the form in which they were written, most enterprises, including agriculture, would cease to function. The difficult aspect is to understand what regulations and to what extent officials are going to apply."

Alena said: In Russia, the communist government failed to make agriculture either a prestigious or profitable area. More often than not, the urban population believed that peasants were poorly educated and ill-cultured. To marry a peasant or to live in a village was humiliating for educated women from Moscow or St. Petersburg. Only the most ugly and stupid women were worthy of it and did it from the misery. It was a stereotype about men who worked in the agriculture. Most Russian women in the past considered true for any country. They tried to avoid such men when choosing a groom. How is your work different from the traditional view of it?

Victusha: "In America, everything is different. This traditional look is extreme. The reality is that most agricultural production is carried out using the so-called "family farm" (which can be organized as a corporation). It is usually led by a well-educated, responsible person, capable of managing millions of dollars. Very large farms are becoming ineffective because the operations manager is increasingly moving away from everyday activities, and small operations cannot produce enough so that owners can accumulate enough capital for growth. "

Alena asked: Do you think that the Americans work a lot?

Victusha: "As elsewhere, some work a lot, while others do not. Much depends on the situations in which people find themselves. But many of them are independent and creative people. However, one unpleasant side effect of American society is that some people are too strongly supported by the government. Such people should simply work, not hoping for a government handout. "

***

Intrigues

In the fall of 1996, the "FBureau" awarded Victor the highest title "The Farmer of the Year". In this difficult time of personal problems and divorce, this news was a bright light for him. At that time, they were living Kentucky, and Victusha joyfully shared the upcoming event with Alena, anticipating their joint trip to his celebration. But Victusha's relatives could not come to terms with his desire for the freedom, new happiness or with his plans to get married again. His ex-wife opened a real war against it, setting his daughters and all relatives against Alena. At the same time, she was taking away huge amounts of money from Victusha and prolonging the divorce.

Victusha's two spoiled adult married daughters took their mother's side and helped her to torment their father, to hurt him in every step. They had lived all their lives on the father's money, and could not have allowed the loss of their well-being, and even less the loss of inheritance. One day they took their father to court demanding to give them more money and some land he owned and paid tax on. It did not occur to them to try to understand, sympathize, take the side of their father, reconcile with his decision about a new life, or at least stay on neutral ground. It would be smarter for them to make friends with their father's new woman, instead of fighting against her. But they prefer to unfairly blame Alena for all discord with their mother, considering Alena to be the cause of the divorce.

And then one day Victusha got an unpleasant phone call in the office of his coal mine. The wife of his youngest brother Nona called. She considered that she had the right to intervene in all family affairs, happily took on various dubious, sensitive issues, and wanted to designate or to teach Victusha how to live correctly. With the skill of a cunning snake, she is used to manipulating other people in order to achieve her goals. So this time, Nona deftly convinced Victusha that he had no right to bring his new woman to his own celebration. It was obvious that such a requirement had already been reviewed and approved by the family council. For Victusha, this was another unpleasant blow, emphasizing his dependence on family money. Having regretfully told Alena about this intrigue with the tears on his eyes, he flew alone to his triumph. A few sad days passed. Victusha came back even more convinced that his decision to start a new life with Alena was the only right one for his whole life. He often repeated to her: "You are the best thing that could happen to me in this life." Now no one and nothing could turn him off a new path.

***

***

Joy

Beautiful, elegant clothes create a good mood, and everything around becomes joyful. And the clothes themselves tell a lot about the nature and life of a person. A person of high culture likes people with well-developed aesthetics, people who understand beauty and notice it. Although they escort a person through the mind, they meet him by their clothes. But each situation requires its own clothing style.

From childhood, Alena was brought up with an impeccable style, and liked neat, elegant people. When she met Victusha, she was glad that he also had a good taste. He patiently listened and fulfilled any of her simple desires. Most importantly, he did not kill her enthusiasm, but, on the contrary, with joy he supported her every initiative.

The most important thing for feeling full of happiness is to encourage, forgive and take care of each other. When people value each other, they try to be pleasant, affectionate and indispensable for each other. Alena wholeheartedly appreciated Victusha's initiative in all he did for her. Everything that happened to her with him brought such a new feeling that she did not cease to smile in response to his unexpected, generous gifts. This brought a feeling of special pleasure; spoke not only of his generosity, but also of his enthusiasm for it. In addition, gifts always create a feeling of gratitude in a woman's soul. And the romantic atmosphere of pleasant surprises is always very erotic, and greatly excites a woman.

Shortly before moving to Kentucky, Alena and Victusha visited Oscar's house. Oscar was Victusha's companion for business at the coal mine. His wife mentioned that in order to "match his high status" Victusha needs to dress Alena well before going there, to the other State. One day he took Alena to a very expensive store, and said that the sellers would choose beautiful things for her. He did not look at the prices, but looked into her eyes. His eyes shone, and Alena's joy was his joy. Her happiness was his happiness. They walked around the store for a long time and chose new outfits. And then, three other saleswomen tried their best, picking up her jewelry and shoes. For the first time in Alena's life, a man wanted to dress her beautifully in his refined taste. It was an incredible adventure and the biggest surprise for Alena. Victusha seemed to her an enchanted prince from a fairy tale, or someone simply unrealistic. Finally, they opted for a strict black dress from "Valentin Couture" and magnificent jewelry from "Christian Dior". Alena felt like a princess, and she enjoyed the complements of the sellers, their attention and smiles. Victusha also ordered a new suit, a beautiful shirt and an original tie. They were both ready to travel to some wonderful social, where they were invited by some new Victusha's friends.

***

Katie

Traveling around the world, visiting wonderful places, we keep in the heart only a few, where we left a part of our soul. Alena used to live in beauty, working in the palaces of St. Petersburg. To feel happy, her eyes needed to find daily beauty. Victusha had once taken her to a small town in West Virginia. Elkins remained forever in Alena's soul, as the most wonderful place.

West Virginia, like Kentucky, had many coal mines. Soon Victusha made new friends from the same business in West Virginia. Among them were the local landowners Katie and Charles Kelly. They also belonged to the high society of Elkins. Victusha and Alena enjoyed their company. Moreover, there was a mine on Charles's land that he planned to sell to Victusha. The proposal seemed to be tempting, and therefore Alena it seemed incredibly suspicious. She thought again: "If the mine is generating income, why is someone going to sell it?" But she did not feel her rights to talk about it to Victusha.

Fortunately, there were no women in Kentucky or in West Virginia who would set Victusha against Alena or who would fight against their relationships. Their mutual friends did not compete with Alena, did not fight with her for the primacy. Therefore, the relationship between Victusha and Alena at that time was almost cloudless and joyful. The aristocrats

Katie and Charles became their best friends.

They both turned out to be surprisingly light and charming people. It seemed that their goal was to create for Alena and Victusha the most comfortable atmosphere in their town or even in their state. Katie was already more than seventy years old, but thanks to the skill of plastic surgeons, she looked very young. But most importantly, she was young in soul and full of enthusiasm. And she also had a wonderful talent: she could easily and delicately create good relationships and maintain friendly relations with a wide variety of people.

The famous great-grandfather of Katie was the founder of Elkins, and many places were named after him. In the center of the city there was a monument called "Man on a Horse" in the honor of her glorious ancestor. Husband and wife Kelly participated a lot in business and social life, as well as in numerous charitable events. They very kindly met Victusha and Alena in their town, and began to introduce them to their friends, business partners and businessmen. Victusha and Alena took part in various charity dinners and business meetings with new friends, shared the respect of the city and business circles.

Katie was a beautiful, attentive and generous person. As lively and cheerful as Alena herself, with a good sense of humor and endless topics for conversation, she quickly became her best friend. With ancient roots and untold wealth, Katie was still not arrogant. Realizing how intelligent, educated and intelligent Alena was, Katie began easily and with a burning desire to patronize her. They were largely two pair boots. Katie drove Alena everywhere with her and introduced her friends. After a cold reception in California, Alena was especially missing warmth and sincerity. But suddenly she found it all in a stranger, in the true Lady Katie. With her Alena always felt incredibly pleasant, and did not want to leave her at all. Victusha also trusted Katie. Once they went to a new shopping, and Victusha easily gave Alena his credit card. Katie was well known everywhere, and in the best shops and beauty salons they were greeted like princesses, enveloped with friendly attention.

Traveling through Virginia, Alena and Victusha stayed at the best hotels where the coal mine queen, Lady Katie, pre-filled their refrigerator with delicious food and favorite fruits. This attention of seemingly strangers was in sharp contrast with the reception by Victusha's relatives. The contrast was unexpected and extremely pleasant.

Soon, Katie and Charles invited Alena and Victusha to a special concert of classical music in their State. For this amazing concert, a special tent was erected in the mountains of Snowshoe. People from different parts of the USA flew there for one purpose: to listen to good symphonic music in a beautiful setting. After this wonderful concert there was a great dinner at the upscale restaurant Red Fox with musicians and the conductor of the symphony orchestra. The invitation from Katie and Charles for Alena and Victusha was a joy. At the dinner, they did not need to be afraid of anyone, no one pressed on them, did not express reproaches, did not create guilt. Their names were next to each other at the table. The guests sitting nearby were extremely polite and helpful. So Victusha was talkative and cheerful. It was incredibly new and beautiful time.

Every time Victusha and Alena were in Katy's simple and elegant house, it was like a celebration. Many people dreamed of being invited there. Katie easily accepted Alena into her circle, having no artificial prejudice against the Russian woman. She entered Alena's heart forever as America's most remarkable woman. It was she who became the beautiful symbol of the country. Once, having learned the amazing story of the unique meeting of Victusha and Alena, their God sent love, and problems they had with Victusha's relatives, Katie recommended that Alena be enrolled at a local college.

Davis & Elkins College was the best place not only to get a good education, but to pass the time before Victusha's final divorce. After listening to Katy's wise advice, Victusha did not hesitate for a minute. He immediately paid Alena's several months of study, including a private room in a dormitory. Alena was in heaven from the opportunity to live at least a little bit in this beautiful place.

***

Golden Autumn

Elkins, founded by Katie's grandfather, was a small, but cozy town, surrounded by the mountains and rich nature of West Virginia. The old, more European architecture of the town was familiar and pleasant to Alena. In addition, several buildings were historical monuments and resembled museums. Some of the old Gothic buildings of Elkins stood on the hills, and when Alena passed them, she felt like in a fairy tale. "Davis and Elkins College" nestled among the forest covered hills. In this beautiful fall, trees were especially surprisingly and brightly shining with colorful paints. Every day Alena enjoyed the magnificent scenery around her, and her soul simply sang. She observed many squirrels running through the open galleries of the dormitory. Sometimes even deer came to the door and waited for some food handouts. She wandered around the neighborhood and collected colorful leaves. Then, she created bright paintings with those leaves and decorated the walls of her room.

The ability to give joy to each other is the main thing for the happy life, and the key to personal happiness. Since Alena was a romantic person, she wanted to find a partner who appreciated her romanticism. Victusha seemed to be just such person. Once he settled Alena at the college, Victusha became much more reassured, and flew back to his ranch in California much calmer. However, Victusha still often needed to be in the neighboring state

134

of Kentucky at his mine and monitor its work. And then, in his small red truck, a happy man was returning to Alena in Elkins for the weekend.

When Victusha visited her, he was amazed at the ingenuity and various inventions with which she was waiting for him, and supported her in all her effort to make them happy. One evening, she dressed in her long, transparent peignoir, put a ring with fluorescent light on her head, and was waiting for Victusha at the window. Seeing his truck approaching, she lit several candles in the room and ran out to meet him. Her desire to surprise and charm was a pleasant gift for him. Victusha flew to her with a huge basket of flowers, with happy eyes and open arms. During all her stay in Elkins, her little room was drowning in flowers.

Flowers were the main romantic and generous gesture. And when the flowers were carefully selected, they stayed in a vase for a long time. This was also a significant sign of Victusha's attention. This meant that the man carefully searched for flowers, spending some time to find the freshest and most beautiful. Victusha loved to repeat: "My goal is your happiness." Alena felt this, and saw it in his actions. They both felt happy because they both loved to give joy to each other. In the afternoon, Victusha and Alena walked around Elkins, and took many photos. They enjoyed the incredibly blue sky and the colorful colors of their first, most unforgettable autumn. Alena was interested in everything around, and especially in the theater.

Her everyday life in Russia was not easy, so she felt the need to often go to the theater. For Alena, the theater was a special event, a celebration of happiness and joy. She enjoyed visiting the magnificent theaters of St. Petersburg. In addition, Russia women have a tradition to dress in their best dresses for a "trip" to the theater. And this exit "into the light" made Alena happy. As soon as she met with Victusha, a visit to the theater became regular. There were several theaters in Elkins where they watched wonderful performances. Also, in October, they attended the "Queen of the Forest" festival. And then they admired a very colorful parade with the fireworks. This fall, near the college, Indians and Highlanders lived, representatives of the so-called "primitive lifestyle." They settled in tents, cooked at bonfires and demonstrated their skills in various crafts. Alena and Victusha visited their camp, asking about life and traditions.

The magic of little Elkins, the old town in the mountains, was also remembered for the fact that Alena was immediately involved in an active public life. Seeing her thirst for the new experiences, Victusha also tried to keep up. Between meetings, their romance continued by the telephone. Victusha called Alena every day, and she told him about her fascinating and such pleasant life in the magical Elkins.

This private college was Alena's absolute joy, and she cheerfully greeted each new day, flying in the clouds with happiness. There was nobody who would send some bad or negative energy towards Alena. It felt very secure and pleasant all the time. Only once she felt uncomfortable. Only one day in the dining room Alena wanted to sit down at the long and almost empty table with the American students. But one very young, pimply boy addressed in an unfriendly manner, saying that she should go to the other side of the room, where was the table for the international students. This confused Alena, but she shrugged off the unpleasant aftertaste of discrimination and went there. When Victusha came to her, he also flew nearby on the wings of love. She never told him any negative feelings about anything there. All her experience at the college was completely beautiful, unexpected and fabulously pleasant. Most importantly, nobody competed with her for anything. She did not need to feel defensive or to protect herself by sending her protective energy around her. It was always very exhausting for her to generate such protection; every time she would get ill or became weaker and weaker. On the contrary, it was the best time for Victusha and Alena, time of their incredible, careless freedom and enjoyment. One evening, December 12, 1996, Victusha expressed his feelings in a short note: "Alena - You are the woman of my dreams and more. You are more than I dare to hope that someday it will be mine. I will love you forever. We will build a beautiful, happy future together. I love you. Victusha".

College

Thanks Victusha's generosity Alena was enrolled in one of the best educational private institutions of America. The high cost of education at this college was the reason that only children from the richest families of America and foreign countries could study there. In order to attract new students, the college created a very comfortable, homey atmosphere. Each student in that place was simply "carried by hand". They treated students the best they could, and tried to please them with everything that was possible. The most prominent professors were invited to work there, and the atmosphere in the college was creative and friendly. The classes were small, and most often three or four people attended the lesson. These were private lessons, with great attention to each student. And it was nice. So, Alena liked to learn English with a select group of classmates. They were all twenty years younger than she, but this was not noticeable. There Alena quickly changed her tourist visa for student status, and got her legal position.

There were many carefree, rich students from all over the world in a very comfortable dormitory, where Alena had her private room. Many of them still spoke English poorly, but were easy in relationships and adored a smiling Alena. Finally, for the first time in her life, she plunged headlong into all the delights of student life. Classmates sought to attract her to their entertainment, inviting her to all sorts of events, parties and to bowling fun. Alena most often refused, saying that she is much older than them, that she has a daughter of their age and a seven-year-old granddaughter. Then they were upset, and in the evening they nevertheless came straight to her room, and persuaded Alena to go with them to some fun event. One young Japanese man, her classmate named Shane was in love with her, and wrote: "Elena, you are a beautiful lady, and I consider you with my blessings."

Victusha left for Alena to use a huge car, and parked it directly under her windows. Alena's school friends were amazed by the generosity of her man. Alena was proud that her friends admired the beautiful car, and asked her to show them what was inside of it. But she did not need such huge car in a small town. She was simply afraid to drive it or to crash into something. At that time, Alena was particularly pleased to just walk along the streets of the wonderful town and around the college. All the shops were nearby. This luxury she did not have in California, and was very happy about this. Sometimes, Alena and Victusha went for two days trip around the area in their beautiful vehicle. But the tourist or forced-camp life did not cause her delight, because this was enough for her in her youth. And to sleep inside the car in the fall was already cold. This car was not completely like a really good "motor home" with all amenities inside, like some Americans had. Also, Alena always preferred maximum comfort with hot water and a shower. But still these trips were pleasant and romantic.

The college dining room with a buffet table was one of the most delightful places there. It had long tables covered with the tablecloths. The dining room furniture was more like it would be in a good restaurant. Every week students of different countries celebrated their holidays or special days in that dining area. In such a day, the entire dining room was decorated in the colors and flags of their country. The dining room waitresses wore the folklore or national costumes of the country whose holiday students were celebrating. For example, when the students from Greece celebrated their holiday, everyone wore Greek costumes and Greek food was served in the dining room. This college had students from Africa, Brazil, Japan, Korea and other countries. Everyone tried to be as friendly as they could with each other, and all were very active and cheerful. Students created their own traditions, sat with pleasure at that one long, unifying table and talked. When someone new appeared on the college grounds, students organized a special party for this person to support and greet him.

A beautiful lady Shane was the soul and the manager of the dining room. Every day, in the morning, she stood at the entrance and greeted each student by name. She, like a mother, found a moment of attention for everyone, asking about school, family or events of the day. She understood that all students were very far from their home, homesick for family, and needed emotional support. This was a manifestation of that benevolent policy of those wonderful people who worked in this outstanding place. The most important thing for them was to make students feel that they are one friendly and large family of the earth. Also, the teachers and guests of the college often came to the same dining room to have a meal or to see the wonderful Art Center or attend a concert.

Another special and spiritual place was the chapel. It was a very interesting building of modern architectural design, similar to a pyramid with a spire and a cross. All college life was governed by the sounds of the bell tower. Alena began and ended her day to the music of the bell ringing and the loving phone calls from Victusha. These were magnificent, magical sounds, bringing hope, filling her with peace and happiness. Every Thursday evening, students came to the chapel to listen to the pleasant music. Also, there they all together sang some songs. Chaplain Laura was one of Elkins' most spiritual and sweetest people. She talked a lot about different religions, church holidays and the Bible. Once, Laura read one of Alena's first stories, noting her thoughts in a notebook that Alena gave her: "Elena, thank you for sharing your story with me. What a tragedy you have overcome! You are obviously a caring, warm person, and I'm glad I met you. I hope your time at Elkins will be useful not only for learning English. But also to make new friends and to know yourself. My prayers are with you and your children in Russia. May the peace of God be with you. Laura. "

"Do not have a hundred rubles, but have a hundred friends." This is Alena's favorite proverb, which faithfully always served her. In Russia, life was impossible without friends, who often were saving her from many sorrows and troubles. In Kentucky, and especially in West Virginia, Alena and Victusha spent the happiest autumn of their lives because fortunately they met good people. All of them clearly saw their happiness, the great love, and kindly supported Alena and Victusha, emphasizing the incredible value of their amazing meeting. And this pure, beautiful feeling illuminated everything around and reflected on everyone. People influenced Alena's and Victor's perception of the reality and their state of mind. On top of that, the magnificent nature and diverse architecture awakened Alena's imagination, inspiring her to create new stories. At that time, for the first time, she began to write regularly short stories in English. She showed these first writing experiences to her wonderful teachers and friends. Many respectful, supportive notes and approving thoughts appeared under her stories, and became a great incentive for Alena.

One of the unique and modest people in Elkins was the talented teacher Trish, who worked in a primary school for retarded children. For Alena, this woman was an example of selflessness. Her father worked all his life as a lawyer, but suddenly he was paralyzed and suffered from Alzheimer's disease. He could not speak, move, understand or recognize people. For many years, Trish took care of him, and was happy with her devotion to a hopelessly sick person. Despite the fact that she was very tired in this difficult work, everyone around saw only her smiling and kind face.

Moreover, she and Alena had many common interests. She asked Alena about her vast and diverse life experience, and Alena read her stories to Trish. They talked a lot about Russia, where Trish was several times. Trish wanted that Alena would help her in the learning of Russian language. In addition, Trish was a volunteer to care for Russian children. During this period, two Russian teenagers lived in her hospitable house. Her large, cozy house was next to the college. Alena and Trish occasionally walked with her dogs, enjoying nature. Once she read Alena's story about stereotypes, and Trish wrote her thoughts: "In your story "Stereotypes", you talked about propaganda and negative stereotypes created in the Soviet era about America. How strong, sad and significant this essay was to me. You expressed the sad circumstances of the universal problem. You made it much more credible thanks to your personal experience. You are right that the topic of stereotypes is very deep. But at least we can discuss it and look for some kind of light. There is hope. "

***

One person, Gene became specially treasured friend to Alena and Victusha. That wonderful person was Victusha's lawyer and helped Victusha a lot in his business. Once he invited them to visit his ranch in KY. At that day Gene's chic estate gathered his friends and their wives from high society of Kentucky. They met Alena and Victusha very friendly, and actively asked her about Petersburg, while sharing their impressions of their recent travels in Europe. Gene even began to correspond with Alena's daughter, who still lived in St. Petersburg. Later, he gladly accepted the invitation to fly to California for the wedding of Alena and Victusha.

Gene was also a big fan of Alena's writing talent. Once he sent his feedback on her story "Freedom for Artists": "I really liked Elena's stories. Elena, perhaps you should create a series of stories about Russian life for publication based on your knowledge. Of particular interest to the Americans will be those changes that have occurred in the life of Russians since the time of perestroika. I find the "Freedom for Artists" to be very interesting and informative. I also really liked the other works that you wrote. You are a very talented writer. And I am amazed that you have achieved so much in the short time you have studied English. Mark, Becky and I look forward to seeing you again when you return to Kentucky. You and Victor can always visit our house. Sincerely, Gene."

This was one of Alena's most remarkable stories about the poor, oppressed Russian artists who went out to sell their paintings during the years of "perestroika". At that time, Alena did not have the opportunity to tell that "perestroika" became a tragedy for many ordinary people, who are largely dependent on the state and did not know how to live independently. Gorbachev's transformation turned into a huge tragedy for a country falling apart under the rigid breaking of old traditions. After the 1990s of this notorious "perestroika," Russia could not recover for a long time to its former power. Only at the beginning of the 2000s, Russia, as it were, rebelled, was reborn, and its new, more independent path began. But this encouraging letter from a senior lawyer and friend of Victusha, his supporting words about the story, Alena often reread later. It inspired her and helped to overcome the ill-will of California dummies, envious women and arrogant women.

Once in West Virginia, Alena met an American who described his personal perception of the Russian events of the 1990s that he had witnessed. "I have always admired the Russians, their minds, souls, their literature, ballet and music. It seemed that in 1991, after so much suffering, they were free. I agree with Alexander Solzhenitsyn that people who suffered from communist rule nevertheless retained their spirituality. However, the West has lost its soul mired in materialism. When you visit empty churches in Europe and listen to the politicized and ideological versions of Christianity that are so common in America, it's hard for the West to see the future, despite its money and weapons. I expect great things from Russia. I expect her to rise, like the Phoenix, from the ashes of communism, and one day will lead the world in many areas. I look forward to hearing music and reading literature, which will certainly be produced by the new revived Russia. And historians will one day cite the inability of the US government to form a strong partnership with Russia as one of the greatest strategic mistakes of all time. Instead of welcoming Russia to the West, the US government regarded it as a third world country. They freed the wolves from Wall Street to help the Russian wolves plunder the assets of the Russian people. This stupid policy continues to this day, which could only be regretted."

This autumn, to Alena's natural cheerfulness was added her overwhelming happiness. Her whole appearance simply glowed with admiration for the town, college, magnificent nature and the friendly people she met there. Maybe this is why Alena, without ceasing, talked about her fiancé with everyone who had ears. Soon everyone around knew that he came to her every weekend. Some time passed, and they began to be invited to various political meetings in neighboring states, where they flew in private jets. College President Dr. Dorothy, learning that Victusha owns a Kentucky mine and that he is the fourth-generation farmer and a landowner in California, also rushed to invite both of them to a society dinner at her home. It was a great honor and only some special people were invited to her beautiful house. This time, dinner at the college president's house was in honor of the famous American political scientist Dr. Richard from Boston.

There Alena and Victusha met the best college professors and respected people from the community. The table was set with many excellent dishes, and everyone enjoyed great food and wine, talking to the quiet music. The landlady Dorothy asked Victusha, who also had the status of the Doctor of Economics, to give a short speech on his favorite subject. The next day, the local newspaper published an article and photos about this dinner, which for Alena was a pleasant surprise.

***

The atmosphere at the College was warm, pleasant, and highly productive. Being a very sociable person, Alena needed to have good communication with people, which had a huge incentive for her creativity. At this college, where everyone respected her, she loved making friends. Living among very young people in the dormitory, she understood that her time there is extremely precious and could end any moment. Alena had a motto: "Time is money." She was in a constant hurry to do a lot of things. Every day she enjoyed doing the homework, and rushed to her classes next morning with joy. Alena was very pleased to share her love for her beautiful city of St. Petersburg with everyone. She could talk about it for hours, showing videos, photos, magazines, postcards, books, photographs about suburban palaces of Russia, and, of course, about her family. Later, while living in California, Alena missed that wonderful city of Elkins, its ancient architecture and magnificent nature. But most of all, she missed her clever professors and friends that she had met at Elkins.

Besides good friends, Alena loved to meet good tutors there. They actively helped her not only with English grammar and idioms, but also with the pronunciation of words. The energetic and knowledgeable lecturers inspired her. She met very high professionals at Davis and Elkins, and enjoyed making efforts to study their subjects. Teachers, like her classmates, were sincerely interested in the history and traditions of international students. So, in the lessons they talked about everything and shared knowledge about their native cultures. It was incredibly important, and helped to overcome the homesickness that every foreign student experienced. Their educators talked about America and the various world events, at ease, without propaganda or pressure, and without political disturbance. Most teachers were highly educated men with doctorate degrees, deep culture and very good manners. In addition, they did not have sexual bias, and they treated everyone very evenly. The unique personality of each teacher, and huge knowledge and friendship with students created a very comfortable mood in the college. Almost all students felt at home there, as in their own family, and this created a very comfortable atmosphere

It somehow happened that all the teachers paid special attention to Alena. At first, she thought it was because Victusha's business partner, Katie, took care of her. But gradually it became clear that friends, classmates and teachers were simply glad to see Alena and be with her cheerful personality every day. They eagerly asked Alena about everything she did, and were happy to hear her incredible life stories. When she felt that soon would be time to say goodbye to them, she began to give them her "memory book", where they wrote down their impressions and thought about their time together.

The statements by her teachers Gwen, Spencer, Villa, and Dean of the faculty Gary were especially valuable for her. Their letters of approval became the main support for Alena for many years to come. Their kind words gave her the strength to overcome many troubles and the unfair treatment of some California snobs, which she later met again. She kept their letters, rereading the refreshing thoughts of her Elkins friends and their faith in her, Alena felt that some good people really could understand and appreciate her deeply. These teachers' letters were the most important stimulus for her smiles and hope for a better future.

One of the teachers wrote: "To my elegant Russian student who sees the beauty of nature and life with her poetic eyes. Best wishes! Mike M. 25-9-96." And another teacher admonished: "Elena, you have a wonderful view of life as "everything is bright and beautiful." And with this attitude you will never make a mistake in life. You are a wonderful student, absorbing knowledge like a sponge. Be successful and continue to study. Gavin, professor of EST, Elkins, WV, 1996. "

English lessons were taught by an amazing professor, Will, a calm and understanding person of advanced years. Will was a walking encyclopedia, and he had a scientific answer to everything. He gladly shared his vast knowledge with his students, and with pleasure watched as they grew in front of his eyes. Before Elkins, he lived and worked in

Washington, DC, and often told interesting stories about his favorite city, showing maps, urging students to visit this city. His first letter in Alena's notebook appeared on October 2, 1996: "Elena! I sincerely wish you a bright and happy future. Your sensitivity, energy, intelligence, and what you understand and cherish, for all True Beautiful, make you an excellent candidate for teaching. I hope someday you will share your talents by teaching others. Good luck. Will. "

One day, Victusha came into Alena's classroom, and she proudly introduced him to her beloved professor. Suddenly, Will said to her fiancé with dignity: "I hope you enjoy Elena's presence in your life as much as I like her presence in my lessons. If she did not have a groom - you, I would marry her." Victusha was pleasantly delighted and smiled. These kind words, uttered by a stranger, cut into the memory of Alena forever with a blazing fire of delight, which then warmed her for a long time.

Another stunning person at Elkins was the director of the International Institute of Languages, the dean of the college, young and elegant Michael. In dealing with everyone, he was incredibly thoughtful, aristocratically polite, and simply an exquisite gentleman from head to toe. A deep sympathy immediately ran between him and Alena. They felt with each other, like two pair boots. He was always very happy to see Alena, and emphasized that the door of his office was always open for her. Alena rarely used this. She was afraid that too close friendship with that intelligent person could lead to something else, and would destroy her relationships with precious Victor. But still she only occasionally dropped in to chat with him about this and that, to share where they had been with Katie Kelly or to ask for advice.

Another outstanding teacher was the professional writer Spencer. His lectures and his conversations with Alena about world literature, even fleeting meetings in the corridors, were magnificent fireworks. He reminded Alena of her exciting and inspirational youth years at Leningrad University. Further in her life, she never met a more energetic and enthusiastic person

146

than Spencer.

Gary, a wonderful young teacher, was especially attentive to Alena, as well as to many other students. He was their best friend and spent all his free time with students, participating in their daily lives. Everyone ran to Gary to talk and pour out his soul, especially if something happened to someone. And everyone knew that he would give good advice or suggest how to do the right thing. One day, he struck Alena with his request to bring her stories to him to read. It was surprising that he wanted to set aside time in his busy schedule, and read, analyze her stories, although he was just a substitute teacher and they met only few times. Once Alena mentioned that soon she would have to return to California and would meet again with the cold relatives of her future husband. Then he wrote to her: "Dear Elena, your style is that skill that any woman can envy. Thanks for taking the time to talk to me. I learned a lot from you and even more than I taught you myself. Gary."

Only one day passed after his note, and for the second time he asked Alena for her notebook and added: "Elena," your style impresses me the most; your lively, cheerful enthusiasm for life, which you express through your stories and your personality. Your style is as individual as your fingerprints. Believe it and believe it is true. With your style, having a little courage, you can easily go through all levels of society, from the most privileged to the most modest, without feeling inferior in one or higher in the other. Never feel the need to borrow another person's style or manners. It will be obvious. Be confident in expressing your style. I notice how people reach out to you and feel comfortable with you because of your style (Gary, Elkins, Wisconsin, November 1, 1996." In delightful Elkins Alena found everything that she loved in life. When strangers met, they greeted and smiled at each other. Every day Alena heard pleasant words of encouragement. Elkins refreshed and inspired Alena. There Alena left a huge part of her soul. It forever remained among her dearest places.

***

Musicians

For the purpose of enlightenment, Elkins often hosted international meetings and concerts dedicated to various nations of the world. So, once Alena was invited to a very unusual concert of Russian music and poetry. This concert was made by completely unique people - Barbara and Gary Zhurstedt. They were virtuoso pianists playing four hands. But most importantly, they were rare connoisseurs and fans of Russian culture.

Even more interesting, they sought to convey their love for this beautiful country to all those who attended their concerts. When Alena came to their concert, they asked her to read for the audience Nekrasov's poem in Russian. They wanted to convey the music of Russian poetry. Surprised Alena (a beautiful actress in the past) did it with great pleasure. Of course, after the concert there was a feast, and they immediately became friends. They maintained good relations for many years. Later, Barbara flew to Russia, where in St. Petersburg she met with Alena's daughter and granddaughter. And a year and a half later, Alena invited them to California to play Russian music at her wedding with Victusha. That day in California, Barbara joyfully wrote for Alena in her book of remembrance:

"Dear Elena and Victusha, it was a happy circumstance (or was it fate), when Elena entered our program at Davis and Elkins College, and we invited her to read Russian poetry. This was the beginning of a beautiful friendship with a beautiful Russian woman. And now, when we met Victusha, we see two beautiful soul mates. I wish you both an extremely happy life together, and may your union also symbolize the possibility of love and trust between the peoples of the United States and Russia! Barbara Zurstedt. August 2, 1998. "

***

Masquerade

Active people, like Alena, have many interesting events in each day. Especially eventful time with Victusha was the first autumn in 1996. At Elkins, the last day of October - Halloween was celebrated on a grand

scale. Strange scenery of the decorations from horror films appeared everywhere around the houses. The very tradition of celebrating this "festival of the dead" with dressing in terrible costumes and "begging" at other people's houses was filled with dark energy. For Alena it

was a completely unfamiliar holiday. In Russia, nothing of the kind was noted, and it was not accepted to "agitate" or bother the dead. But there was something interesting about the celebration in the USA. It was possible to attend a masquerade, wander around the villages in costumes, and the children received free sweets.

Alena and Victusha received an invitation to a Halloween costume

ball at the college. It was the first masquerade ball in Alena's life. The morning of this day they began with a trip to Morgantown. Trish invited them to meet her new Russian children, and help with the translation of the rules of living

conditions in her house. Alena could not refuse her best friend Trish, and went with her to give parting words to these teenagers. And Victusha spent the whole previous day driving his truck, hurrying to Alena from Kentucky. Although he was still very tired, and would prefer to spend time in bed, he did not want to be alone in the dormitory, and went with them to meet the Russian boys. In addition, after this meeting, he decided to take Alena to a special store in order to find costumes for the evening event.

It was a very long, but fun day, and the first part of it they spent in the shop. For Victusha, they found very quickly the costume of Count Dracula. And Alena took quite a long time to find something not traditional, not beaten, but something completely new and special. She was incredibly interested in measuring various fabulous dresses and going out to Victusha to show him how beautiful she looked in each of them. And the store owner tried to please her. With each new dressing, Alena, like a good actress, absorbed the image of the costume, and her behavior and manners also changed. It was an exciting game. Despite his tiredness, Victusha patiently waited for her new transformations, smiling in surprise at each of her new images, and giving the girl wonderful compliments. Alena was completely happy from the knowledge that she had a new entertainment: to please Victusha with unusual characters who created different costumes. In those moments she felt like Cinderella before the ball.

Finally, Alena picked out an unusual long dress that shimmers with gold and illuminates it with her light. Victusha understood and appreciated her good taste, as well as the high quality of things. But quite a lot of time had already passed in this store, and he was happy when she finally came to him in a gold outfit. This time in the store with the admiring face of her fiancé gave Alena the feeling that she was as if in a dream.

Most women believe that love is manifested in the generosity of a man. At least, men have to give some flowers and gifts for the main holidays and memorable events, like birthday, International women days, Valentine's Day, New Year and Christmas. But the generosity of a man is manifested not only in how much money he spends on a woman. Alena was sure that the generosity and love of a man is manifested in his words and attention to a woman. Victusha paid her really great attention, she responded with a good attention to him. All of it was feeding their love.

People say that one cannot judge a book by its cover. But any woman likes to go shopping and dress up. Victusha's generosity, his love and patience gave her an incredible feeling that she is a true woman. It was evident that he was proud of Alena and all she did. For a long time, he had a thirst for love and tenderness, hidden deeper under the guise of harshness and fear of rejection. Finally it began to blossom in full force because of Alena's love and care for him. And Alena's feeling for him only flared up because of his attention to her, and his generosity. At that special day in the store, it seemed to her that she suddenly became some incredibly beautiful creature, worthy of the greatest love and adoration. Victusha whispered softly: "You are my Golden Queen." He really did everything possible for Alena to be his queen in their first Halloween masquerade and in life in general.

This costume ball was held in a historic building, similar to an old castle located in the colorful mountains. All the mysterious surroundings, castle decorations and an exciting concert made this holiday exceptional. Everyone came in costumes, and the masquerade ball was well organized. Everywhere something unusual and fascinating was happening under the tender music. Some unknown for Alena scenes from some fairy tales were performed. Various contests were held after a delicious dinner. Among them was a contest for the most original pumpkin carvings, where many participants received nice awards. At that evening, Alena also received the award for the most elegant costume and the title of "The Golden Queen".

At the end of November Alena saw the snow falling down in Elkins and became sad. She never planned to live in the USA in a cold climate. Wherever she lived, she always missed the marine climate of her childhood the most. She wanted to be on the sun, swim, sail her boat and doing everything else what she did when she lived in Gelendzik by the sea.

Although Elkins College was an amazing place to get an excellent education, Alena did not want to live permanently in the cold climate of West Virginia. In addition, Victusha was very tired overcoming a long journey on his truck from Kentucky to visit Alena for the weekend. At the same time, his mine did not generate income, but gave only trouble. Altogether, in Elkins, Alena and Victusha spent a fabulous autumn, meeting many wonderful people. It was the best time of their lives. But in December, the paid semester was ending. It was the time to decide what to do next. Then, Victusha decided that it would be better for them to live permanently in California, where Alena could continue to get an education at the local university. Besides, Southern California was located by the Pacific Ocean. Victusha had land, a ranch and a house there. Therefore, it seemed to be the most suitable place for her future life with Victusha together.

***

Gemini

Victusha was born under the sign of Gemini. Gemini has a double nature, and this was soon noticed by Alena in Victusha. Alena's daughter was born under the same sign, and she knew the difficulties of such people. One day Victusha could be in a good mood, and the next day - he would be as a completely different person. His Zodiac Sign belongs to the group of air signs that possess observation, curiosity, logical thinking and wit.

In the horoscope it was said that such people go through life with the confidence that everything around is beauty and grace. They are irreplaceable and responsible individuals who understand that excessive kindness kills independence, and excessive care inhibits spiritual growth. But they also have an amazing mixture of pragmatism and idealism. Their

152

naivety is manifested in relation to themselves, and not to the whole world. Unfortunately, they do not see the world as a mirror of self-knowledge, and they are not able to objectively evaluate themselves. It seems to them that moving forward helps to get rid of past problems. They pay too much attention to unimportant trifles, without thinking about the consequences. As a result, they are helpless and defenseless in the face of some kind of big problem or disaster. A fire, a flood, an earthquake, or something else like that will lead them to a long stupor and inactivity. These people like to disassemble something, reassemble and repair, as well as solve puzzles and puzzles. Living with Victusha, Alena had a chance to verify the correctness of his horoscope.

"The larger the person's soul, the deeper he loves," said Leonard Da Vinci. On the first look, it seemed that Victusha was not a typical American, but was a special person. He strove to become the best friend and life partner of his young wife Alena. His long and sincere interest in Russian culture, learning her language, trying to pronounce some idioms, reading the English versions of some Russian books made him much closer to her. She really highly appreciated it. Although Victusha did not like to talk about himself, he gradually revealed himself more and more. Alena finally found out that besides being a fourth-generation farmer, he had graduated from a prestigious private university, received an excellent education and got his doctor degree in economics.

By his nature and upbringing Victusha was a very open, sincere and polite person. His main character traits were modesty, generosity and honesty. And also he had a great sense of humor, which often saved him from being too serious about himself, about people and life circumstances. When trouble happened, he smartly tried to push it away, leave it behind, and distract himself with some positive things or being alone until everything would settled down. But sometimes it seemed that like all Gemini, he often hid his head in the sand, instead of facing the truth and fighting for his rights and justice. For his noble, pure soul and kind heart, Alena called him "the last knight of America."

Among his talents, the most remarkable was his amazing ability to listen attentively and patiently to people, to understand and support them. But there was a deep problem for him as for a very sentimental man. Delving into someone else's life, listening to other people's requests or complaints, he felt obligated to somehow help such a person. Women (including his daughters) as normal predators, right away saw his too trusting nature. They quickly tricked, circled him, and wrapped him around their finger in their effort to get what they wanted. His trustful nature and nobility was used by his ex-wife in a divorce, as well, and got a lot. His sweetness people used against him when they called him on the phone. They were always very energetically persuasive him of the "profitability" of their business, only with one goal: to get his money. He got angry if Alena tried to help him to understand it.

***

Long Road

In December 1996, Alena sadly said goodbye to all the friends of her beloved college in Elkins. Then, she and Victusha drove to his mine in Kentucky. There they loaded two trucks with everything they wanted to take to California. Victusha tried to foresee any surprises during the long way to California in advance and even acquired two speaking devices (intercoms) to have a connection with her on the road. But before their long journey Victusha did not have time to teach her well how to operate them, and during the road Alena did not have the courage to use them. Soon Alena and Victusha set off on a long journey through several states to the Pacific Ocean. They had to drive five to six hours a day, with a stop only for the refueling cars and for spending the night in roadside hotels. Apparently Victusha thought that having a driver's license was a sufficient guarantee of Alena's driving skills. But in Russia, Alena had her own driver, and rarely drove a car herself. Even after gaining American driver's license, she rarely sat behind the wheel of a car.

Besides, Victusha's trucks had a manual gearbox and several speeds, which Alena did not understand. Alena never had the experience of driving such a car. To everything else, she did not know how to navigate the terrains or to understand traffic signs and could not read the maps well. Moreover, both trucks were huge, long, loaded to the top, and the rear window was completely blocked by things loaded into the trunk. Due to the fact that the truck was heavily loaded, she did not see what was happening behind. Only the side windows gave her some view of the road. But she turned on the radio with optimism, and for some time enjoyed the music, rejoicing in the new adventure and proud of Victusha's confidence. Victusha drove quickly ahead, and the back of his car was the only landmark for Alena.

They began to drive out of Kentucky in bright sunny weather, but after a few hours, in the state of Tennessee, heavy rain began, and the fog dragged on the road. Alena no longer saw Victusha's car. The road was narrow, with only two lanes in one direction. Huge, heavy trucks raced alongside, splashing mud on Alena's car. She shied away from them to the very side of the road, driving her truck almost along the very edge of the highway. The car window wipers worked like crazy. But still they could not cope with the heavy rain and dirt from the cars rushing past. She felt desperation, slowing down more and more. And then she stopped completely. But passing cars began to scream horribly, drivers rudely cursed, leaning out of the windows and showing her the middle finger. But Alena did not understand their gestures or bad words. She was lonely and felt bitter. Realizing that she was lost, Alena turned into the first exit that came away from a noisy highway. Panic despair seized her. She was in a foreign country, in a heavily loaded car, with no a very good English, no legal documents, and without any knowledge of where she was going. After sitting a little and looking around, under the rumble of rain, she began to try to reach Victusha on her intercom.

Finally, he responded to her desperate cry, and Alena was relieved to describe where she had roughly stopped. He arrived very quickly. His calmness and kind words consoled and reassured the frustrated girl. After driving a little more they stopped for the night in some God-forsaken place. Alena was unhappy to sleep in a cheap motel, in a not-so-clean room smelling of cigarette smoke. But there was no way out. Not getting enough sleep, still terribly tired, Alena got up at six in the morning. She again drove her truck alone for about six hours, barely seeing the fast-racing car of Victusha in the distance.

At one of the parking lots, Alena already felt incredibly weak from many days of tiredness and poor sleep. In addition, she caught a cold, barely stood on her feet, and was in a bad state of mind. All the charm of their magical autumn in Elkins began to become foggy. In huge desperation and very disappointed in the difficult journey, Alena quietly asked Victusha if they could leave these two damned vehicles somewhere, or to hiring professional drivers to take the trucks to California. But Victusha replied that it would be too expensive, and these two cars with old things are not worth it. This journey lasted a terrible seven days, and looked like a test their relationship. Alena already had no strength to react to Victusha's reassuring smile and his kind words. She just bit her lips and drove her huge pickup.

***

BOOK 5. California

Before their official registration of marriage, Alena and Victusha lived happily together for six months. Alena dreamed of being the main person in the life of her husband. At first, she thought that Victor could make her as a part of his former family. In order to achieve it he would try to talk to them describing all good stories about her and about their joyful life together. By telling them something wonderful that Victusha and Alena had all the time, sharing with them his love for her, his relatives might start to appreciate his new life and Alena, as his wife. Then, they would form an opinion about her according to his kind words, because Victusha really loved her and was really very happy with her. But it did not happen. He did not talk to anybody about his happy life with her. He was afraid to contradict them and their opinion, which was formulate by his ex-wife and his nasty daughters. Mainly, he did not want to upset his relatives telling them, that they were wrong.

During her travel from West Virginia to California, Alena consoled herself with the various dreams and pleasant expectations that lay ahead. Arriving there, Victusha rented for them a small one-room apartment in the humble Mexican area of San Marcos, not far from the university. The apartment was in a special complex for others not yet full-fledged students and poor Mexican families. But it had a nice back yard, well-groomed alleys, and a community swimming pool. So, Alena was pleased with the opportunity to swim, and did every day.

They furnished this small apartment with everything they brought from Kentucky. Victusha sometimes complained that in his house on the ranch there was a complete mess, nobody cleaned it well, and no one was doing anything for the comfort those who lived in it. Alena out of habit created coziness in their new little place. And he was very pleased with her effort to make something from nothing. Although the old-fashioned furniture from the mine sometimes annoyed Alena, it was still pretty nice in their cozy nest. The money that Victusha left her for everyday expenses, Alena used to decorate a little their modest place, or to please him with some small surprises when he would come back to her in the evenings.

Seeing Alena's homesickness and slow adaptation to California, Victusha began to take her to various events. A new active life and communication with new people were very important for Alena. Her soul longed for movement, beauty and spirituality. To bring some positive moment into their life, and to make it more stimulating, they soon began to go to different dance classes and make new friendships. Victusha told her about everything around, helping her better understand the events and customs of people. Gradually Alena began to come to the conclusion that she could feel better if she became more tolerant of the new environment. In California's dry and hot climate people wore very simple clothes. So, she also began to wear more comfortable dresses. And it made life easier, as well as reducing spending. The main thing was that Alena tried to find something interesting to do, something that would give her joy and meaning to life. But she could not find what to do and how to live. She felt like she was hanging in the air with no base.

But Victusha's coal mine was getting worse and worse, absorbing all his savings. He was forced to continue to borrow huge amounts from his parents with the interest above it to pay them. Having learned this way of doing things in his family, Alena was very amazed. In Russia, parents usually helped their children without any contractual conditions, without receipts, but simply because of their love or sense of duty. Here, the importance of the money was in the first place. In addition, the lengthy divorce proceedings, the dividing of his property, and expensive lawyers continued to empty Victusha's bank and his pocket. It was evident that he suffered terribly. But it was not his habit to blame someone for the loss of his money, or to complain infinitely about endless problems. In this situation Alena did not want to spend any of his money on anything, or on something that she could live without. Although Victusha gave her his credit card, she did not feel free to use it, because her name was not on it. So she did not ask for anything, and did not do anything without his consent or permission.

Seeing his gloomy, upset face with the deep wrinkles, realizing how hard it was for him to deal with all depressing events, Alena decided to help him. She gave him all her personal savings that she had brought from Russia. He was grateful to her, and immediately invested ten thousand dollars in her name in the special bank. But after a few months there was nothing left of this money, because "the stock fell." And the other twenty thousand he used to pay a huge salary to his secretary at the coal mine. But Alena was not upset losing her only money, only one security she had. Victusha swore that he will return all her money, and even more. And she sacredly believed him. She loved him and felt his love. It was the most important thing in life.

***

One day Alena received a sad letter from her homeland, from Gelendzhik. A woman wrote that she was caring for her helpless grandmother, who was left alone and her Moscow sons did not come. She was left to her fate. A neighbor noted that she learned from Alena's letters that she had a very good job and a very good marriage in America. The woman asked for some help, and begged Alena send her five hundred dollars to pay for the dental work she needed. But by this time, Alena no longer had a penny of her money. Of course, she could ask Victusha for this money, and he might not to refuse her. But Alena did not dare to ask him about it. Recently, in Kentucky, she already asked Victusha for help with some money to her friend Dima. Victusha lent him a thousand dollars, and Dima soon returned it. But again, to ask for money from the eternally sad Victusha, and even as a gift to an unknown woman in Gelendzhik, Alena did not find the strength in herself. Much later, Alena bitterly regretted that she could not send this money in payment to those who cared for her only old, helpless relative. The burden of this excruciating inaction (as many others before that) and failure to render assistance always worried Alena's conscience, and did not let her sleep at night.

***

From San Marcos, where they still lived together, every morning at 5:30am Victusha drove to his ranch to monitor everything that was happening there and to work in his home office. Also, still, twice a month, and for two weeks, he flew to his coal mine in Kentucky. Returning back, he periodically still pleased Alena with flowers and small gifts. They spent a fabulous time together, closing their eyes to everything that existed outside their apartment.

When Victusha was in KY again, left alone in the foreign environment, Alena somehow coped with her longing and daily problems. Although all the Mexican shops were pretty close to her apartment, it was necessary to have a car to get to a good grocery supermarket. But soon Victusha's father bought a new Cadillac for his wife, and gave his old, huge Chevrolet to them. It was a pleasant surprise, and Alena got at least some kind of transportation for daily use.

America generally has huge cars everywhere, and this old Chevrolet was just a giant among giants. Soon Alena was not able to park it in the narrow parking space allocated to her in the residential complex, and crushed it slightly on the bumper. She was terribly afraid to tell Victusha about this accident out of the blue. In Russia, it would result in huge expenses for the repair, problems with the workers at the repair shop, and in big inconveniences, with long weeks of waiting to fix it. But, to her amazement, Victusha was not even upset. He just quietly said that the car insurance would cover most of the expenses. It was unexpectedly new for Alena, because she just began to learn about the insurance topic. To have different kinds of insurance was very important in the country, even though they were like a spider web. Only some poor people did not have it. But in the situation with the crashed car, for Alena something else was more important. Victusha's calmness in all critical situations gave her an incredible encouragement to trust him more, believing in his kindness and love.

***

***

Compatibility

Some wise man said that "every person must eat a crumb of dirt (a pound of salt) before he dies." Once Alena and Victusha, while walking in the San Diego park, went into the Museum of Natural History. There they saw a huge and seemingly unremarkable stone. Surprised that a simple stone stands in the middle of the room, they walked around it. They were even more surprised when instead of a dull stone on the other hand, a sparkling surface of a purple mineral appeared to them. It was mysteriously and confidently shimmered with the inside of the beautiful gem. It was a miracle. Alena and Victusha stood near this gem for a long time, thinking and talking about miraculous transformations, unexpected

161

turns and vicissitudes of fate. In life, so often, something is not at all what it seems at first glance. The same is in the relationship of people. While living together before the marriage, Victusha and Alena found out that they have many common interest and deep compatibility with each other. It was good.

Each couple has its own reasons for living together before marriage and work on their relationships. Living together before marriage is like work to open hidden treasure. If we want to find a gem, then we must work daily to cleanse the surface of the stone from everything else, superficial, superfluous, getting to its precious essence. Good sex, passion and love are not enough for a successful life together. Living together before marriage, we are deeply exploring a partner so that in the future there are no unpleasant surprises. When the right choice is made, it is comfortable for people to just be quiet together. But in general, good relationships inspire each other, and make it easy for each of you to do your favorite business.

Indeed, communication between people is the only real luxury. It seems important that two people will have common views, level of education and interests. For example, if one partner likes to talk about philosophy or art, while the other does not understand or is not interested in this, then they will be bored with each other. In any case, you need to find common topics for conversation. Active time together also means communication. John Gray, in his book Mars and Venus in Love, wrote: "I urge him to tell me what he thinks. In good human communication, there is a need to share your thoughts with your partner, and instead of just listening to your partner, you need to actively listen to him, to delve into what he said, trying to understand and support".

Interestingly, one day Alena lost her favorite wristwatch and was very upset because it was Victusha's first gift. She decided to share with him her sadness about it. But to her surprise, he did not blame or scold her, as she expected from her past with other men. He simply warmly tried to console and reassured her, saying that this was just a thing. And in life there are other, really important things (like human health or devotion). Later Alena found his treasured gift, and was very glad about it. But mostly she felt grateful to him for showing his love, wisdom and understanding. This example proved that he really valued their relationships. They were very compatible, and their open communication and sharing thoughts was the key to the successful marriage.

Alena found an exact description of their relationship with Victusha in the book "Mars and Venus in Love." It said: "We have tools to express our needs, feelings, likes, dislikes and format, so as not to cling, not to perceive things too personally." Seeing that she can trust Victusha, and having learned this, Alena became really happy, blossomed and began to smile unceasingly. And, learning to trust him, she saw how he flourished, too. They were different, and his previous life path was also not easy. But they did not have to force change, but only to adapt, find common ground and compromise. It was their path to mutual happiness.

From the previous relationships, Alena knew that happiness is the result of daily and intensive work with each other. This work means thoughts, actions, and behavior should be directed with an eye on the partner. You must ask yourself: "What can I do today to make it pleasant for him, how to make him happy and comfortable with me?" If these questions are in the center of your attention daily, then you are on the right track. Living together for even short time would show if you are compatible with each other. But also it will demonstrate if you have the opportunity to continue to grow in love and polish our relationship as a wonderful gem. Alena and Victusha were lucky to have all above, and grew in love more and more happily together.

***

University

Having moved back to California, Alena had to adapt again to the new conditions. It was time to look around and figure out what to do next. The new life was overwhelming with many different and new things to do and to learn. Alena wanted to find a more significant lifestyle than she had before and which might be closer to what she had in Elkins.

First, she decided to go to the local university and continue her education as a form of adaptation to America. She had already received high education and a diploma from one of the most prestigious universities of Europe. In addition, she traveled a lot, had vast experience of life and deep knowledge in many areas of art, culture, history and literature. Somehow, all this manifested itself in her communication, posture, style, and clothing. But she felt a need and the time to be more comfortable in her new life. She wanted to continue to study English, and also took a class in the Mexican language and the history of America. A new state university was recently built in several blocks from their apartment. The building was designed in a modern style with small windows. But for Alena the "architecture" of the building resembled a prison. The university courtyard was completely paved, and there was not a single green bush or a tree around. Under the hot sun this courtyard glowed white. At breaks, students tried not to go there. In the afternoon, everyone ran headlong to the parking lot as fast as possible to get to the car.

However, the atmosphere at the public university and the attention to the students was not the same as it was in Elkins. Probably, California's dry and hot climate had a negative and flammable effect on both students and teachers. The snobby students and not very cultural teachers were different from those people whom Alena was lucky to meet in West Virginia. It felt like everything that Alena was respected for in Elkins, here caused anger and irritation from her classmates. Those around her, with a few exceptions, felt her superiority and independence and were terribly jealous of her. Alena saw this, and during the breaks tried to read something or study subjects without talking to the classmates. And after class she hurried home to the love of Victor waiting for her. At the same time, most students did not like that she did not participate in their conversations and parties, or that she did not spend any time with them outside of class.

Once, Alena, keenly feeling the unfair attitude of some Americans towards Russia, tried to challenge the absurd opinion of one teacher about the history of her homeland. The teacher never has been abroad, and her opinion (obviously) was formed by the media. In addition, she did not tolerate any contradictions to her life views, and considering herself to be the ultimate truth. After her public debate with Alena, who clearly had superior knowledge of the world history, this teacher simply fiercely began to demonstrate her dislike of the Russian student. When she entered the classroom, she shone with hatred, tried not to look and not notice Alena. This teacher was afraid of Alena's objections or adjustments to her superficial knowledge.

During one year of staying at this educational institution, Alena met only one friendly and pleasant person. It was a teacher of American literature with the name Magda. On September 27, 1997, Magda wrote in Alena's notebook: "When I think of you, Elena, I am amazed at your determination, zest, courage, but mostly your strong thirst for knowledge. I saw it in the last semester, and it opened in me the same bright spark that almost died. You, it seems to me, have always been a seeker of knowledge. Another reason that I will regret that you are leaving the university is that you inspire and excite my mind. It makes me very happy. I do not often get such an opportunity for growth in the classes with foreigners. I did not lose sight of the fact that you are inherently genius, with your mind and soul, and very sensitive. And I'd say to your Victusha (he seems to be a very nice person): "I hope that you understand what a gem you have in your best half." And to your classmates who could not understand and appreciate what you tried to say in the lesson (even when you went beyond the scope of the topic), I would say: "It's a pity you lost a lot, not paying attention to Elena's ideas."

PS. To give you inspirational advice is like trying to find a New Year's gift for someone who has it all. Be patient with those who are walking under someone else's drum (about the situation in the classroom), whether they are blowing into someone else's tune. Give at least some chance, it would seem, the most senseless things (like group work in the classroom). Most importantly, always remain just yourself. Good luck, Elena. You are a bright, radiant presence. Best wishes to you. Magda."

Victusha and Alena lived together in San Marcos one year. His ex-wife still was living in his house on the ranch, and they could not settle there for another year. Soon Victusha got an opportunity to arrange their life more comfortably by renting a spacious house in a beautiful place called Bonsall. After several month there, they wanted to celebrate two years from the day they met, and began to prepare for their real "wedding dinner," which they had not yet celebrated.

***

Consideration

But a long time before meeting Victor, Alena was sure that her wonderful daughter Lila and granddaughter would be re-united with her in the United States. She tried to help them to improve their lives as well. Alena tried to tell her husband as much as possible about the culture and traditions of Russia. For example, the "International Mother's Day" on March eight was one of the important holidays for Russian women. On the eve of this holiday, the delicate Victusha, wanting to please Alena, wrote a very warm letter to her daughter in Petersburg, expressing himself as their future parent, and not as a stranger. This sensitive attitude towards her

166

family made Alena love him even more. This is what he wrote:

"Dear daughter Lila! Congratulations on the International Mother's Day! I hope you are in a good mood and your weather is improving. I know that it's cold in your place, but spring will come to you soon. Remember that we love and think about you, and look forward to seeing you this summer. I am always pleased to read your warm, sincere postcards and letters that you sent to us. Your selection of verses that you recently sent, I really enjoyed. In addition, the cards were beautiful and significant, and of very high quality, better than many of the cards that we find here. They show that you spent a lot of time and effort to find something special to make us happy. Your letters show that you love us and think about us, too.

Your mother tells me about her telephone conversations with you, and translates some of your letters. We like the photos you sent to us. Many of them Alena placed on the walls of our apartment, where we constantly see them. She also talks about Marina and describes your life in St. Petersburg. Now I think I know you very well, despite the fact that we have not met.

My friends, Charles, like Gene, were very impressed with your smart, touching words. Both of these men are very kind, wise and experienced people. Any of them will be a good husband or, in any case, will be a good friend. Try to keep friendship with them. Remember that smart people want spiritual communication. So, good English would help. Please be diligent in learning it, because it will greatly contribute to your future success. I sincerely hope that soon you can find a caring and loving husband for you and father for Marina. Be patient, courageous and decisive in your search. We are always happy to hear something about you, and you can always be sure of our support. Take care of yourself! With Love, Parents. "

***

Finally, Alena's daughter Lila and granddaughter Mary were able to get out of Russia. For a short time they lived within two hours from Victusha and Alena, but soon they were forced to leave that place. Victusha again showed himself as a truly noble man and an understanding husband. He accepted them as his new family, and agreed that Alena's daughter and granddaughter settle in the same house with them in Bonsall. Then, for more than ten years Victusha, as a good step-father supported and provided them with everything they needed. He gave them the opportunity to settle in a new country. Lila and Marina were well brought up. They were very attentive and caring to their new relative. For Alena, Victusha's kindness towards her only relatives was the most important thing in the world. All of them adored Victusha for his generosity and took care of him.

Memory

Each person has some precious memory or something valuable from the past that he cherishes. For Victusha, one of these precious things was the Teddy bear of his childhood. Once in the house of his mother, Alena saw a photograph in which two-year-old Victusha hugged a Teddy bear and smiled happily. At that time, this toy was twice as large as the child. That photo was done on New Year's Eve of 1943. In his childhood Victusha loved to pinch and bite the bear, and this is why the Teddy bear had shabby sides and bald patches. Later, Alena put that photo in a frame and hung it on the wall of his bedroom. Every day he could see his happy smile at that photo of 1943, when every day was magical and careless. Alena hoped that the good memory about carefree childhood would delete some wrinkles and sadness from Victusha's face. The photos from the youth emphasized the transience of life.

168

While looking at the old photo of Victusha with his Teddy bear, Alena also thought how wonderful it would be if somebody carefully preserved at least one toy from her childhood. She did not have people in her childhood who would love her enough to give her the toys. When someone gave her a present, Alena wanted to know what was inside of it. In the house of her grandmother, she lived in a permanent atmosphere of secrecy. From very earlier years she had a strong desire to open all secrets around her. From her irrepressible curiosity she took apart every toy she ever had. Watching her doing it, people did not understand what the reason was behind it. They wanted she would keep her few toys in a pristine condition. But Alena could not help herself, and they stopped giving her anything.

During the hard time of the divorce, Victusha suddenly found his teddy bear in the trash can. Obviously somebody at his house wanted to hurt sensitive and sentimental man, or to erase his childhood memory. Victusha found his teddy bear, and brought a precious toy to his cozy home with Alena. Victusha's childhood Teddy bear found his happiness in their house in Bonsall. Alena looked at him and thought that Teddy had a very kind and wise heart, because he had experienced many difficult trials. She wanted to console him a little. First, she put a necklace around his neck, and he no longer looked abandoned. Then, she decided that Teddy could be even happier if he had a girlfriend.

Before Easter she bought him a pretty Bunny rabbit with a little hare in a small basket. Seeing them nearby in an armchair, Victusha and his Teddy were pleased with the gift and the company of new friends. The Bunny was sure that she was magnificent in her flower hat and bright dress. She looked like a very young, vibrant foreigner, and she liked the company of Teddy. They had a lot of things in common in the past and in the present. They immediately fell in love with each other at first sight and made friends. Bunny and Teddy were always sitting next to each other, hugging each other, talking to each other day and night, and no longer felt lonely or abandoned. During the Christmas or new Year periodically Victusha took his Teddy bear, looked at him, analyzing what has he done in the past and what else he could do good to support his only love and be happy with his Alena.

***

Bell

One day, Victusha and Alena went to a meeting of the "FBureau" in a special big ranch. To Alena's surprise, the owner of this place was a man named Bell, who founded the famous Taco Bell Restaurant. People often stop at the popular "fast food" places to get the food home without leaving their car. Alena especially liked the "Taco Salad". This completely unusual ranch "Bell "was built in an amazing way. Alena saw streams and waterfalls there, huge glades of bright colors, a lovely, small lake with colorful fish. To the astonishment of all guests, there was a miniature railway station with many small trains, which were the owner's hobbies. Alena and Victusha, as well as other guests, made a short trip along this miniature railway. Traveling in an almost toy car, they saw many rows of vegetables and Mexican workers looked after it. Alena was interested to know that this magnificent ranch was open to the public. Every day anybody who wanted to buy vegetables, ride the railroad or just find out something interesting came to it.

Then, a wonderful dinner was organized at the Bell Ranch, and Victusha, like some other participants, made a short speech. Alena realized that the whole situation in California with farm enterprises was very different from other countries. The new president of the "FBureau" expressed his hope that the government would not continue to interfere in the affairs of landowners. Then everyone went to ride in a van, which was pulling by a tractor. Everything was very nice and fun. Alena dream to have something like that in Victusha's ranch.

It was a hot day, and walking and talking to good people was cheerful and pleasant. At that day, there, they met with one of Victusha's friends, Congressman Bill. They asked him if he could help for Alena with her Green Card. She had lived in America already for several years, but still

170

did not have it. It was promised to be done. But Alena has been waiting for it almost ten years.

***

 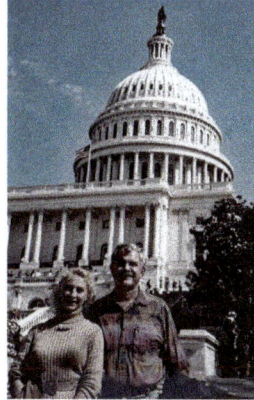

***

Little Things

Victusha often invited Alena to attend some fun events and concerts in Escondido, a small town nearby his house. Once in the lobby he saw his ex-wife. To Alena's surprise, Victusha energetically headed towards her. Then, he politely entered into a short, seemingly meaningless small talk. And then, suddenly, but proudly introduced Alena to her, as his future wife. Alena, being a very sociable and also polite person, out of kindness, smiling, cordially extended her hand to her. But she turned coldly to the other side, like she did not note it, and stepped aside. It was a strange case, after which Victusha tried to never again mention his hated ex-wife.

At the same time, for several years in a row, Alena still tried to establish good relations with his hostile daughters. Many of Alena's attempts to make friends with them, her gifts, effort to talk, greeting cards for the holidays, all were unsuccessful. They hostilely responded with silence or neglected her friendliness and efforts. Under all those circumstances, Alena also understood well that selfish children could be very cruel and ungrateful. At every family meeting, they plotted, whispering secretly, and accusing Alena of destroying their former family. Feeling intuitively all of this, understanding and seeing these intrigues, Alena, at the same fearing to appear impolite, did not say anything to anyone in her defense. But Victusha did not notice anything and was silent, continuing to attend stressful family meetings out of politeness. After such meetings, they always both were upset and saddened. Alena felt like Cinderella, and did not understanding how his own daughters could be so cruel and ungrateful.

Once ex-wife realized that he would never return to her, she began to delay the divorce by all means, preventing Alena and Victusha from legal marriage. There was no end to that process. Their material and financial demands only increased. Victusha was ready to give away everything in order just to start a new life. Finally, his lawyer recommended that he carry out a special procedure for a complete divorce without his ex-wife's consent (bifurcation). In such case, they could continue to do the division of his property later. Victusha agreed immediately. To force her to leave his house on his ranch, and by court enforcement, he bought her a house for half a million dollars not far from his land. The court ordered him to pay nine thousand dollars a month to his ex-wife, and forced him to buy life insurance. With this money, they all happily lived, never needing anything. But the human soul cannot live cherishing malice or hatred. Ten years later, his ex-wife fell ill and died in terrible agony.

***

So often most women are trying to give men good advice, while teaching them how to do things their way. They want to adjust him for themselves. But men might start to listen to them when there will be a moment of silence. The success of communication is guaranteed with the ability or gift of listening. It might be trained by willpower. When people live together, there are no little things or trifles in their communication. Living side by side, they learn the secret habits that they usually hide. Here it is necessary to "keep an eye out." It is quirks and tricks that violate the harmony of relations. If you want to be happy and keep your relationship, it is best to try to adjust, find compromise, and try not to do what annoys another person. For example, if he snores, and a woman cannot sleep at night, then she needs to have another room for a night's rest. In addition, it would be nice to know in advance if he is sloppy, and scatters his things, leaves the room in a mess, or if he does not like to wash his hands and leaves dirty dishes in the sink. All this can annoy the «neat» woman every day more and more.

The smallest things ("the devil in the little things") can tell you if you are compatible with your partner. The old saying goes: "Clothing makes a person." And another saying teaches: "Don't judge a book by its cover." But the color, quality and style of a person's clothing will tell you more about him than all his beautiful words. All you have to do is look at his wardrobe, and it will be a complete characteristic of the person. Then you will understand his habits, lifestyle, and decide if you can put up with it.

Happiness is when the chosen partner can share another person's joy. Of course, it would be nice if both could enjoy the same entertainment. Such couples enjoy relaxing together, traveling, sharing their free time without being bored. Collaborative fun, like nothing else, brings people together.

***

 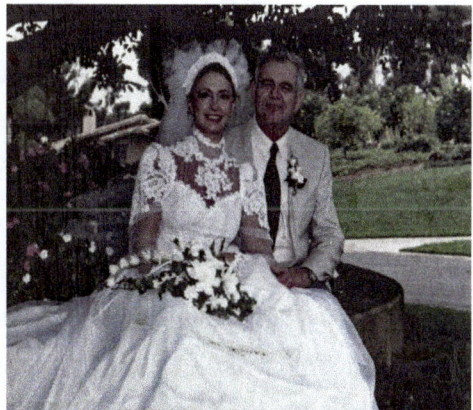

Registration

Alena dreamed of having a happy family life with Victusha, where he would share with her everything that he had. "I like California more and more, I am glad to live near the ocean and to be Victor's faithful, devoted friend and wife." When Victusha finally got his long-awaited freedom, one evening he made an official offer to Alena asking her for a "hand and heart", and presented her with a beautiful diamond ring. The next morning, they applied for the formal marriage registration, and sent out an invitation to all members of his family for the celebration. But no one answered the invitation, and nobody sent congratulation or greeting to them.

For the day of the marriage registration only two their friends, immigrants from South Africa, Robin and Aiden, came to participate in it. They were successful and friendly people, and wanted to help Alena in the new country. Victusha rented a beautiful white dress for Alena. While seeing his bride in all her glory, he simply glowed with joy. His friends and insurance agent Aiden and his wife Robin came to participate in the ceremony, and took many beautiful photographs. During this marriage ceremony Alena, as well as Victusha, repeated after the official the holy words of the oath: "I, Elena, will take you, Victusha, to be my husbands. I promise to be your faithful wife, in good and bad times, in illness and in health. I will love and honor you all the days of my life."

Alena and Victusha were deeply grateful for their touching care and support. Aiden and Robin took care of all the details and even gifts for the wedding day. Also, these two wonderful people after Victusha and Alena's marriage ceremony ordered a pleasant dinner in a good restaurant in Santa Fe. Their gifts and care were a surprise and joy for Alena.

Shortly, to Alena's great surprise, Victusha insisted on publishing the announcement on December 28, 1997 in the local newspapers. He felt that the whole world should know about this wonderful event of their legal union. So, according to the CA traditions it appeared in different Newspapers. For Alena, the public announcement of such an intimate event was not only something completely unusual and new. For her, it was like an oath of allegiance to Victusha, a confirmation of his serious intentions for a long and happy life. The newspaper ad was pretty detailed and included some biography facts.

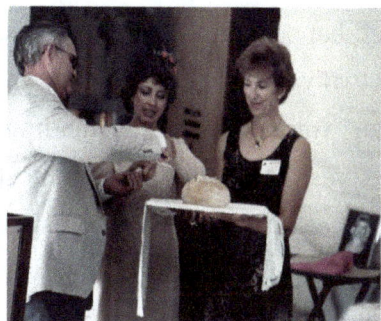

***

Celebration

In 1998 Alena and Victusha organize a beautiful event to celebrate their two years from the date of their miracle meeting and the anniversary of their marriage. They sent invitation for a special a piano concert and a special dinner, which they hold in a fabulous restaurant.

Alena and Victusha did not have a special wedding reception on the day they got married. But they dreamed to have it sooner or later, as a fairy tale with amazing surprises and beautiful gifts. Then, Alena craved to go to Hawaii for their amazing honeymoon. Therefore, one day, they decided that it is time to celebrate two years of their life together, and sent a beautiful invitation to friends and relatives. It started with a meaningful epigraph: "I am a word, and you are a melody. I am a melody, and you are a word." And then followed: "We are pleased to invite you to our slightly belated wedding reception on August 2, 1998. What could be more important in a person's life than a good relationship between a husband and a wife? No amount of money or a successful business can bring as much satisfaction as love and a good relationship. It gives inspiration and makes life complete. Sometimes people seek such luck all their lives, and do not find. And others have the courage to start a new life if they were lucky to meet a harmonious and close person. Indeed, "better late than never."

Usually the most important events between a man and a woman take place in the little things of everyday life that no one sees or notices. Accomplishments in feelings are more important, than in visible, obvious events. The most important event of our life happened in 1996, when we were lucky to meet each other. During these two years, we created our own home, where our hearts found love and peace, warmth and understanding, where we can relax, and where our love lives. Our special and most important time is our present. We value our present, as well as our dreams, plans and hopes. Love is patient and kind. It does not insist on its own, does not irritate and does not offend. Love carries everything, believes everything, hopes for everything, endures everything. Love never ends. We will go hand by hand our whole life with love and understanding."

The girlfriend of Victusha's middle brother referring to employment did not come to their reception. For the celebration of Victusha and Elena two years anniversary, they received warm congratulations only from three people. One of them was from their recent acquaintance, Bill Horne, senior Senator San Diego. Another was a special greeting from St. Petersburg from the loving daughter Lila. Also, Barbara and Gary Suhrstedt, the virtuoso musicians, whom Alena met in Elkins, wrote: "Thank you for sharing with us the special joy of your love and your home. Elena, you have brought into my heart a deeper love for the rich beauty of Petersburg and Russia! Together with Victusha you created love, which, like great music, speaks like a universal language. May your friendship, as well as your love for each other, become even stronger in the coming years! "

***

Guests

The loyal friends Robin and Aiden took over the entire organization of the reception on August 2, 1998. They were active assistants in every detail. During the dinner Aiden was the master of ceremonies. His wife

176

Robin helped to conduct a special game for the bride and groom. According to the old Russian tradition, the newlyweds were asked to break off a piece of bread, dip it in salt and treat each other. This ceremony meant that you have to go through difficulties and joys together, hand in hand, not betraying each other.

Victusha's Kentucky lawyer came to this great dinner. But it was especially remarkable that even Alena's Elkins friends, musicians Barbara and Gary Shurstad arrived to give a special concert in their honor. Alena and Victusha sang the old symbolic song about immortal love, "Shine My Only Star." Then there was the dance of the newlyweds, which was joined by several couples. Several of Alena's recent friends from the "FBureau" made pleasant speeches in support of the hosts.

Elena opened the event with her speech, which started: "My dear, wonderful Victusha! My home is in your heart. "You are my heart's twin. My first thought in the morning, And my last thought at night. You are my soul's mirror, the only one who truly understands how it is with me. I wish I could put into words the depth of my feelings for you. When I think about the good times we've shared, and, yes, the difficult ones too, I feel simply and quietly grateful to have found you." "I love you for all you've given, the warmth of your caring. I love you for all you've meant, the joy of our sharing. I love you for all you are - my life, my love, my everything."

After that, it was Victusha's turn and he gave his speech that he wrote in Acapulco on May 4: "With an attitude like that, how can I help but love her?! When I came across her picture and a short description, I saw a happy, energetic aura around Alena's face. I thought here is a person who loves life, can share everything with me, and be cheerful in any situation. At the same time, I feared that one so attractive would have many suitors, and wondered what my chances would be. Finally, I remembered the adage about seizing the brass ring when it comes up while riding the carousel. I summoned the courage to attempt to grab the ring — I sent to her a short letter with a picture. A miracle happened!! Two years ago, on August 7

I was waiting in LA airport for 7 hours while INS bureaucracy finished checking her documents. There were a lot of people, so I told her that I would be wearing a cowboy hat.

Fortunately, I was the only one with a hat like that. My anticipation was growing, and I couldn't get any information from the airline or the INS. But I intuitively felt that we were waiting for each other our whole life and right now time was irrelevant! These 7 hours mean nothing--soon we will be together forever. When she finally came out, I didn't see her until she came up behind me and said "Victusha? It's me, Alena. Let's go." We've been going ever since.

I tried made her happy by doing all things that she was accustomed to and liked. Yes, we have real true love. Our relationship is so big joy, and happiness lives in our home where everything reminds us of some events in our life together. Since we absolutely trust each other and are open and free with each other, we enjoy every minute of our life together. Trust creates our good mood and inspires our life. She shared all difficulties with me that I had these two years and was my angel-keeper. She is all my heart, all soul, my best friend, partner and companion.

Here in a foreign (for her) country she has only me - her whole family and her whole home. So I will forever try to give her all my love and caring. I will with all my strength give her happiness that she deserves. Now, our love is growing as the really great and true treasure. We are happy, and invite you to share with us our happiness.

"I'm glad there's you to talk to and brighten up my day, to share my thoughts and understand the things I do and say. I'm glad there's you to laugh with me at ordinary things, to show me what is special in everything life brings. I'm glad there's you to be with and I think it's time you knew how happy you have made me - how glad I am there's you! I love you for all you've given, the warmth of your caring. I love you for all you've meant, the joy of our sharing. I love you for all you are - my life, my love, my everything."

The biggest surprise for everybody was a special entertainment. Being fans of Russian culture and art, Barbara and Gary made an unusual gift for Alena and Victusha. These two piano virtuosos played a four-handed Russian music concert. But it was not just a concert of beautiful music. They also showed slides of Russian paintings and told amazing stories from Russian history. All guests were delighted with the surprisingly intellectual and interesting entertainment that no one expected.

During the dinner Alena asked people to leave their thoughts in her "Book of Memory", and many guests wrote something pleasant for the hosts. However, nobody among Victusha's relatives expressed any greetings or congratulated the hosts, and nobody brought any gifts. After the dinner, Nona suddenly declared to Alena's face that they arrived for the dinner only with the purpose to "see other members of the family." They did not stay for the wonderful piano concert. When Alena came up to Victusha's mother, and asked if she should call her "mother", like the other daughters-in-law, she was told that "I'm not your mother. Call me by name only."

From that moment, Alena realized that it would be best to stay away from all of Victusha's unfriendly relatives. None of the women in Victusha's clan wanted to express their friendly participation, respect or understanding. At family receptions, no one asked them about anything, or wished them happiness or prosperity. It seemed that they emphasized only that it is not good to go against the opinion of the family.

Alena always dreamed only of the tranquility of her heart. She needed a faithful, loving husband who would first of all stand by her. Only his respect and admiration fed her. Most importantly, she wanted him to be on her side in all situations. Their house has become a quiet oasis for their peaceful, quiet relaxation. Those who considered Alena to be a culprit of the loss of their money and inheritance could not appear there. For a long time at those meetings, Alena continually supported her husband, tried her best to smile at his relatives, and politely conducted simple conversation. For many years, Alena tried hard to be pleasant to all of them, wrote them greeting cards, trying to making friends with them. But she did not meet any reciprocal interest or respect.

Soon after their formal "two years marriage celebration", Alena and Victusha left for Russia, where they got married in the main cathedral of Leningrad. And then they went, like pilgrims, on an unusual journey along Ladoga Lake to a holy monastery on the Island of Valaam. This year 1997, Marina went to her first grade of school. It was important for Alena to be there with her granddaughter to celebrate this special time. Victusha was happy to share that wonderful time with his new loving family.

***

One day she decided not to go to any his family gatherings, and Victor did not want to go without her. It brought him some grief, and at the same time, it brought some peace to their relationships. One year passed. Once on a Mexican vacation, Vic wrote a letter to his relatives, but never had courage to send it to them. Maybe if he would send it, they would treat his new wife better. "I silenced for a long time and did not talk about my private life with anybody. I was sure that my family would treat my future wife Alena with all respect and kindness as she deserved by her intelligence, good manners, openness and wonderful personality. Alena is so thankful and appreciates for any small things that happened in her life that we can only admire her! She tries to do something good for everybody. Only for one year here Elena achieves great success, accomplishment that any other women can only dream about. But we did not get one word from you about her writings. However, I know that you found time to read whispering, scuttlebutt, chitchat from my ex-wife. Misfortune, Alena lost her parents very early and she dreamed to find her family among my relatives. I'd like to believe that she will be an equal member of my family. She has so many merits and virtues that some Americans never had or will have. Besides her high education and open mind, she has very high moral principles, ethical grades and high quality nature.

Furthermore, Elena is a wonderful thoughtful mother and careful grandmother. Also, she has kind heart, creativity, pure beautiful soul, wonderful spirit and character. Here, in the USA she already has many friends who love and respect her, who call her "our sunshine," because she is always very amiable, genial and friendly with everybody. Moreover, she is a good cook and our apartment is always clean not like my own house. The most important things for me that she takes care of me so gently and fondly, so much devoted to me and so much helps and supports me with whole her wonderful heart and soul that I love her very much and don't have any secrets from her. She is my best friend, my partnership and she is one woman about whom I dreamed whole my life. We are happy together and I don't allow anybody to destroy our life and our happiness.

As you know, nobody is perfect, and everybody has own past history, do we? I hope you did not expect that I would choose a virgin woman without background? Show me one and I will laugh! I wanted a wise pretty woman with big life understanding, experience and knowledge. So, take her like she is, but she is very good by herself. She truly loves me. I know it, I feel it, I see it every day, and she knows perfectly how to really love a man. It is our prerogative with her to decide how we should live and with whom, about whom we will take care or what to do and how to build relationship with a whole world. I am sure that I have my own rights to do my own way, my road, and build my own relationship with people by myself.

***

Path

Once upon a time, constantly overcoming various problems, Alena well learned one important rule of happiness. She tried really hard to follow the wisdom she learned.

When you see something beautiful, share it with your loved one. Then your joy will be doubled. Even if the other person does not respond to your generous efforts to make him happy, still share the joy of everyday beauty with him. Having seen even the simplest, small miracles around you, share this with the person who lives with you. Your effort to share joy will fill you with happy feelings. Your own sense of joy will cleanse your soul and inspire you to something beautiful. Then, everything around you will shine with more joy. Of course, it would be better if the one next to you would be just as responsive and empathize, sharing your enthusiasm and joy. Then happiness could grow and become twice as strong.

Only when love lives in the heart, is life illuminated by a beautiful light and becomes meaningful. Physical passion alone is not enough for a happy marriage. Love implies understanding, patience, openness and honesty with each other. Honesty is an important thing in any relationship, and especially in marriage. This is what gives it strength.

A good marriage will be successful only when partners are attentive to each other every day. Every day you need to find time for each other, to do something together, to dance, to talk, to walk, to go to the beach or a theater. Trust is the most important characteristic of a good relationship. Friendship always unites us. It is a process of time and exchange of experience, and it does not happen quickly. True friends are people who stay with you during all the storms and hardships of life.

Under the burden of time, physical beauty would change. It changes under some negative experiences, dissatisfaction, and troubles. But life is full of the most wonderful surprises. Where a person knows how to maintain good, trusting relationships, the value of kindness, the beauty of the soul and eyes, there remains forever comfort and joy. A man can easily make a woman feel that she is loved. The main thing is to be able to laugh kindly at your own mistakes or the mistakes of your partners. This laughter will remove old grievances and free your heart, fill your soul with the magic of love and forgiveness.

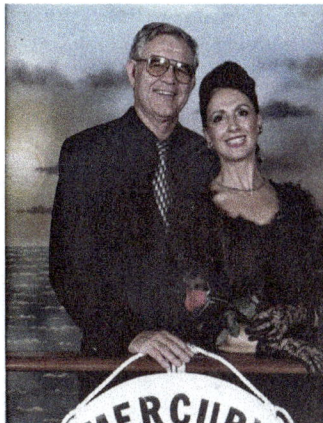

***

There is a special type of rich men who, at the very beginning of a "happy" relationship, would conclude a "Marriage Agreement". Most often, such man follows the mercenary or vengeful advice of his relatives who hate his new wife. There is no single woman in the world will be a devoted wife to a man who made a "Marriage Agreement", where a woman is intentionally deprived of all property and has nothing under her name. Even the strongest initial love in this situation is doomed to defeat. Everybody needs some freedom to be who they want to be. And in marriage, a man and a woman should be equally dependent on each other. They should be dependable for the spiritual, emotional and physical needs. Men and women who live in a calm harmony, in the trusting marriage, actually live much longer than single or unhappy people.

Everyone, in the end, understands that happiness is the result of daily hard work with each other. This work means thoughts and actions aimed at your partner. You must ask yourself: "What can I do today to make something pleasant for her, or how to make him comfortable with me?" If these questions are daily in the center of your attention, then you are on the right track to the happiness. "Good marriage means the difference between a happy and unhappy life." The most important is to make everyday efforts to improve your relationship with your partner. Your long-term, pleasant relationship is the stability that will lead to the success of everything else.

 **

***

Hill House

Once the day came when the division of Victusha's property with his ex-wife was over and the ranch house was vacated. His "ex" took out everything she wanted, down to the smallest detail. No matter what, Victusha was immensely glad to get rid forever of his hated past. He had a loving companion of his life, his lovely Alena, and cloudless happiness that he had dreamed about. He trusted Alena infinitely. Every day he was convinced that he had made the right choice. One day Victusha said: "My house is now your home. All that I have is now yours." Every woman dreams about these the most important words, and they deeply touched Alena's soul.

Around Victusha's house and down the hills there was a beautiful ranch. Alena loved the open space. Since childhood, she enjoyed magnificent nature and loved to spend time in her grandmother's garden. Now she was glad that Victusha's citrus plantations were at the bottom of the hills. "A new place means new friends and new adventures," thought Alena, and began more deeply learn the lifestyle and habits of her husband.

Victusha's rather large and completely custom house was built back in the 1980s. Then in California, the size of the rooms was limited, and the house was more like an unusual Mexican hacienda. Despite the large size of the house, there was no spacious, open space in it, where everyone could get together, sit and chat. The layout of the house, its style, small rooms isolated from each other created a sense of disunity. It felt as if someone specially invented or intuitively created such house in a way that people would not often see each other. It was strange, but roomy. When Alena moved in it, she thought that probably the hardships of the German prison experienced in Victusha's youth had a great impact on his attitude. It reflected in the house design.

The main decoration of the house was made of solid dark cinnamon oak. The columns supporting the ceiling, all cabinets and the doors of the rooms were from the same oak. The floor was tiled with the large and also dark brown Mexican tiles. A long corridor was stretched along the ground floor. It resembled a street with the wooden doors leading to several small rooms. In addition, even several antique furniture some time ago belonged to Victusha's relatives, were also made of oak. The high ceiling of the corridor was decorated with the exposed wooden beams. Several huge and impressive chandeliers hung down, creating an illusion of a castle.

The old house had several problems. The main thing was that the house was poorly ventilated in the past, and an unpleasant, obsolete smell came from its walls. In addition, from the grief experienced in it and desperate longing, it seemed that this sad house was filled with negative energy. On the very first day, Alena broke her leg, and walked in a cast for a long time, thinking what this could mean for her future.

When the house was finally freed from the scandalous tenants of the past, it was necessary first to clean it of all living creatures and insects, which also lived there for a long time. The main door of the house looked directly at the dusty, dirty, not asphalted yard, waist-high, overgrown with tall grass. There were no flowers or bushes around the house. The inner emptiness, joylessness was reflected in every detail of the house and in its surroundings. The lazy and careless people who lived in this house for several decades did not bother to plant anything around it. There was not even a small garden there. Only some groomed palm trees, sadly shook their dried branches, trying to survive in the wild, unspiritual desert. Accustomed to riding on Victor's back, the former inmates of the house simply did not want to work, to improve, or to create beauty around them.

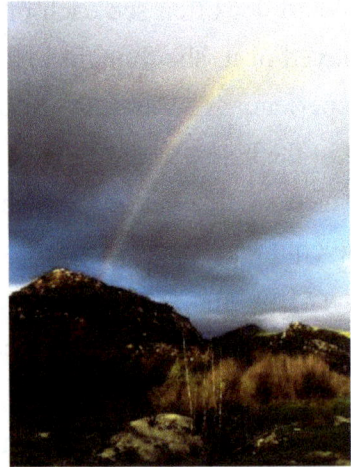

***

The place for the house was wisely chosen on a rock, and the house took on the outline of the hill on which it stood. Going down the hill, the house created several levels, which added variety to the life of its inhabitants. Several stone stairs led up and down, giving the impression of a complex layout. And many steep steps set up the possibility of additional forced daily exercises. However, the fact that the house was built on a high hill was its main advantage. From this hill there was a wonderful view of other nearby hills, road lanes and the ever-dry river below. As far as the eye could

186

see, Victusha's plantations of avocados and citrus trees extended. Many rows of tangerines, persimmons, pomegranate, apple and other trees grew there. From the eastern side, orange and avocado plantations were leaving the horizon, creating an incredibly pleasant picture and joy for those who looked at it. Although, on the other hand, the big, dark brown Lancaster mountain was closing the perspective, creating a very strange feeling of the limitations of all things in life.

There were no paved roads around the ranch. Huge clouds of dust rose around, when somebody was driving up or down the main road, filling the house with it. This dust quickly accumulated on the furniture, on the floor, on all things inside the house. Since Alena had asthma in the past, that dust was a big problem for her, making it difficult to breathe. Moreover, it was necessary often to clean the house. Victusha was kind enough to have

a local Mexican, hired for this hard work. Most parts of the huge ranch were neglected, and needed a lot of repair. Due to the dry climate of California (as the former desert), walking around on the dusty, bumpy roads did not bring any pleasure for Alena. Despite the many green and potentially beautiful spaces, the ranch looked groomed and, most often, simply desperate or even abandoned. For most of the year, always dusty roads were in a deplorable state. There was no particular control over the work of the Mexicans or any special care for the ranch. Support of the vast territory of the ranch was expensive. The fruit plantations had a very costly irrigation system, and poured a pretty penny. In November the heavy rains eroded the roads, and it was almost impossible to leave the ranch. The, Victusha got on the tractor and tried to restore the blurry roads, making new ones. It was his hobby and pleasure. But the tractors often were broken and it was more and more difficult for not young Victusha to fix them.

However, the isolation and the vast space around the house were of undeniable, rare value. It was very special place, and a very different from all the others, "ordinary" Americans who lived under his hills. The most pleasant was that the spring or summer mornings always started with the singing of birds. The nightly silence was broken only by the howls of jackals and coyotes, hunting rabbits by the river. Only twenty years later there was the development of small villages and some comfortable settlements at the bottom of Victusha's hills. Then, the noise of several highways laid nearby was more audible near the house. But it was a distant, some kind of unreal noise of someone else's civilization, or something that did not violate the idyll of a ranch isolated and remote from all the fuss.

There were many benefits of living in so isolated place, away from noise of the city streets. When Alena and Victusha feel like they need activities, they participated in the local different perromances or go dancing.

Alena got a lot of comfort from her dogs, from her work in the garden,

and a beautiful sunsets. In the evening, they watched the rabbits or squirrels go out to eat something in the garden. They have long lived there, hiding from the dogs under the bushes, and happily breeding there. A rabbit father often comes to the garden from outside, and supports his growing family. There, under the bushes, squirrels share the space with the rabbits, pleasantly and peacefully spending time with them. Later at night, the pack of the hunting coyotes roars with the piercing screech in their hysterical excitement to catch their food. They are chasing the less fortunate little creatures living behind the hedge of the garden. Then, Alena takes her gun and shoot from her balcony towards that sound, trying to help the victims to escape. The garden world is full of wonders.

Alena, who was not able to sit in one place for a long time, began to buy shrubs, flowers and trees, improving the area around the house with all her passion. Soon, her son-in-law Romen became her indispensable assistant. Romen flawlessly, with pleasure was taking part in all of Alena's endeavors. The yard, garden and vegetable garden soon acquired amazing beauty because of his immediate help and hard work. In love with Alena and flying on the wings of happiness, Victusha gave her complete freedom to restore and renew a half-empty house. In order to somehow escape the gloom of this strange place, Alena gladly repainted the rooms in all the colors of the rainbow. Sometime after moving in, she enjoyed to decorate this house. They bought several new items that later always reminded them of their happy time together. But Victusha was an economical man. While investing in many different businesses and supporting different people, he did not have a desire to spend much money "in vain" for the improvement of his own surrounding or the house. Loving Alena, who was accustomed to the Spartan lifestyle in the past, did not like to object to him, and put up with everything. She just dreamed that one day they would have another, their own home by the ocean. And yet it happened twenty-two years later. But it was a new page in their life.

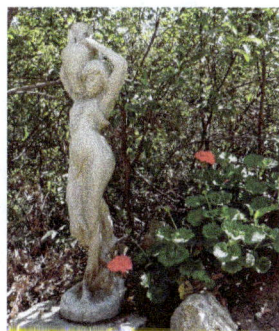

***

Alena was a creative and artistic nature, a craftswoman for making fairytales with nothing. She always tried to make a difference in the life of the old ranch and their home with Victor. Fate sent them to each other, and gave the time for pleasure. Alena dreamed that she and her husband would feel like a one united team. Having similar views and principles of life, Victor happily supported all of her undertakings, bringing them to life. They had practically enjoyed the similar dishes, sometimes visiting good restaurants. They loved to listen to the classical music while traveling by their car, and often went to museums. They were also brought together by evening walks around the nearest hills with dogs.

The main thing was to find something that the husband and wife

would do together. Alena and Victor loved to travel and devote some time for that joy. Calm time on the neutral territory, in a small cabin of a ship, without any negative influence of others, gave them a great chance to adapt to each other's habits. These happy trips enriched, inspired, and motivated their lives. Once, to Alena's great surprise, Victusha easily and cheerfully agreed to go to the ballroom dancing classes with her. It was Alena's long-standing dream, and finally it also came true. Alena's soul longed for beauty, spirituality and constant movement. For her, the most important was to do something with her husband, and the most fun was to dance together. At first, she thought that besides a beautiful and devoted wife, she probably needed to manage this estate. But then it became clear that Alena's special involvement was not required in anything. The creative nature of Alena needed a lot of new impressions. She used to work with a large number of people, and yearned on the isolated ranch, wanted to chat with her friends on her native language. Then she came up with the idea of creating her own dance school and holding charity concerts. Their house had a huge garage, and Alena covered its cement floor with a special coating for the dancing. Students began to come to them, and life became even more fun. Soon she was carried away by the Argentine tango, became the master of this dance, and completely dragged her husband into this new passion of hers.

A generous and sympathetic person, Victusha was also an excellent teacher and helped Alena to master the computer, at the origins of which he stood. Wanting to perpetuate all their fascinating moments of life, Alena shot video clips of everything that happened in their life. And then they edited these home movies together. Most importantly, they tried to  do everything together: they worked on the ranch, swam in the pool and looked after the garden. Sometimes, they spent wonderful evenings to the quiet music by the fireplace, reading or discussing plans for their new cruises and trips. When Victusha got them a beach "candy" house, it was the most wonderful time to go there, to stay in the beauty, enjoying the ocean breath and relax.

Having enough free time, Alena continued her self-education, mastered new programs on the computer and created her own website. Then, she wrote and published her articles on the history of her hometown on her blog. Then, it was the time, when she began to write and publish her own books. To get a deeper familiarization with the local agriculture and business, Victusha began to invite her to the meetings of the "FBureau." There all good people met Alena very friendly, and she, in turn, was proud of the chance to become Victusha's real assistant and like-minded person. Alena actively participated in the work of this organization until the leadership was changed there.

Their family life at the ranch gradually improved and became quiet and routine. Victusha liked to wake up very early and worked in his office at the computer all day. And in the evening he went to the third floor of his living room to watch TV. At the bottom of the house, Alena had her own living room with a fireplace, where there was also a huge TV. Sensitive and caring Victusha got for her several Russian television programs. It was at least some consolation for Alena in her eternal homesickness. The main comfort in isolated life on the ranch was her shepherd dogs. Their dogs were true, faithful, silent and always loving friends. With them, she talked about everything that bothered her. And they listened to her with joy, trying to figure out how to comfort their mistress. All the love and devotion that was lacking from people, Alena got from her wonderful dogs.

But still, from time to time, she became depressed, and then with the great effort of will, she looked for some new activities and consolations in the different accomplishments. Her faithful Victusha patiently and silently tried to wait for her mood swings, and always forgave her emotional overloads. Alena also learned to make compromises, while taking care of her wonderful husband. Most importantly, they traveled a lot, and Alena especially loved cruises, which brought a great diversity to their life. During the cruises they were especially close to each other, and their life was quite active and pleasant.

***

Energy

Once in childhood, Alena's grandfather took her to climb to the top of the famous maintain under the name of Morhotsky Range in Gelendzhik. There they suddenly discovered a huge ancient construction "dolmen" with a round hole in the center. There were several such "dolmens" around Gelendzhik Caucasus Mountains. The most amazing thing was that many

192

centuries ago, someone had amazing skill so smoothly and correctly to carve stones of enormous size. And even more surprising was the fact that someone managed to put these multi-toned whoppers on top of each other, creating houses or vaults.

To the left of that structure "dolmen" Alena saw a bush of her favorite wild blackberry. She was very surprised by these berry bushes,

which so rapidly and merrily grew high in the mountains. She rushed to it, despite nettles around the bushes. Approaching them, the eternally hungry girl began to eagerly pick delicious black and some still unripe red berries, not paying attention to the thorns. This amazing berry was as tasty as it was on the ditch near her grandmother's house.

At that time, her grandfather Minai took photos. Later at home, in his hidden behind the house photo shop, he developed the photos. Then, on one of the photo of the "dolmen" he wrote by using an old special print. "Gelendzhik. The ancient stone house of the ancient heroes. "

Many decades later, in memory of her childhood, Alena planted a bush of blackberries in her California ranch. Blackberry was her favorite berry, and it looked just like in the photograph of her grandfather Minai. She planted it near the metal net of the fence, which enclosed a huge hill near the house. That fence was along the main road and covered a special

territory for her German Shepherds, running in the garden. By planting it she forgot about the surging energy of this lavish and mysterious plant.

The irrepressible passion and energy of the blackberry knew no barriers. There were no restrictions or prohibitions for that bush. And after a year, the blackberry already filled the whole fence, stretching 100 meters in all directions. It began to violently break through the fence further, not asking anyone for any permission, and in spite of any obstacles. The blackberry threw its branches far ahead, and then, reaching the ground, immediately clung to it and sprouted. It looked like it had Alena's energy and character.

And in the spring, very quickly beautiful little white flowers appeared on the bushes, and then berries popped up. The berries also ripened quickly. Alena collected them every day, but the new ones immediately reddened on the bushes, and the old ones blackened. She collected daily a whole bucket of berries, competing with the birds, but the blackberry did not end. They only hid under huge leaves, trying to stay longer in their native home. When once Alena saw it, the pictures of her childhood immediately came back to her, and the kaleidoscope of events has spun.

"Ah, these black eyes - captivated me," dear grandmother Anna sang quietly and somehow very thoughtfully, recalling her beloved, forbidden in the USSR singer, Petr Leshchenko. She carefully looked back at her husband, Minai, a former retired major, fearing that he would hear her song and scream to shut it up. Although there was no stranger in the house, and this was already a "thaw" of the 1950s, the old fear of Stalinist terror lived nearby. This deep slavish fear made one look around at any conversation; speak in a whisper or slip of the tongue. Grandmother Anna, despite her husband's prohibitions, taught her granddaughter the lyric songs of Petr Leshchenko, which she herself knew well. His songs were full of longing for Russia.

And then, sixty years later, in her American ranch garden, Alena suddenly remembered these songs, and sang them with her grandmother again, but also in a low voice. And the blackberries sang it with Alena by the voice of a beautiful singer Petr Leshchenko, tortured and killed by the Bolsheviks.

"I am not walking on my mother's land anymore. A gloomy cold morning wakes me up, and in front of me are foreign fields. I am now far, far away in a foreign country. I miss my homeland, the Russian fields. In the distance, in the blue fog, I see the golden poplars. But I cannot relieve my pain without seeing them again, or without seeing the blue beloved eyes."

Alena was sure, that when people love each other, they have the energy of blackberry and could service anywhere. They could build a very strong house at any place on the Earth…It could be as strong as those "dolmens" on the Gelendzhik Caucasus Mountains…

***

Author

The author, Alena has created many fascinating books in Russian and English, and published them in Europe and America. Among them, it is worth noting several funny books about the lives of cats and dogs, about monuments to beloved animals. Also, her wonderful books about Argentine tango or about the famous Ukrainian artist Valeria Bulat (her ex-husband) cannot be ignored. Moreover, her historical and biographical trilogy about Gelendzhik, memories of her hometown and people who lived there in the 1950-1990s are unusually interesting.

The author has many years of experience in various fields of education, literature, theater, dance, cinematography. She especially enjoyed the work of a tour guide, traveling with tourists around Russia and the Baltic states. She also shared with people her love of art and knowledge of the museums and palaces of St. Petersburg.

During the years of "perestroika", she had her own successful business, which gave her the opportunity to travel around the world. After several marriages, she found her true happiness in California. There she opened a dance school, was the producer of many shows and charity concerts. Her new books are also written there.

***

Copy Rights

***

ISBN-13: 978-1-950311-64-4

978-1-950311-64-4